THE LAW OF ADOPTION

by

Margaret C. Jasper

Oceana's Legal Almanac Series:
Law for the Layperson

Oceana®
NEW YORK

OXFORD

UNIVERSITY PRESS

*Oxford University Press, Inc., publishes works that further Oxford University's
objective of excellence in research, scholarship, and education.*

Library of Congress Cataloging-in-Publication Data

Jasper, Margaret C.
   The law of adoption / by Margaret C. Jasper.
      p. cm. -- (Oceana's legal almanac series. Law for the layperson)
   Includes bibliographical references.
   ISBN 978-0-19-533902-4 (clothbound : acid-free paper)   1. Adoption--Law and
legislation--United States--Popular works.   2. Adoption--Law and
legislation--United States--States--Popular works.   I. Title.
   KF545.Z9J374 2008
   346.7301'78--dc22   2007042502

Note to Readers:

This publication is designed to provide accurate and authoritative information in regard to
the subject matter covered. It is based upon sources believed to be accurate and reliable and
is intended to be current as of the time it was written. It is sold with the understanding that
the publisher is not engaged in rendering legal, accounting, or other professional services. If
legal advice or other expert assistance is required, the services of a competent professional
person should be sought. Also, to confirm that the information has not been affected or
changed by recent developments, traditional legal research techniques should be used, including checking primary sources where appropriate.

*(Based on the Declaration of Principles jointly adopted by a Committee of the
American Bar Association and a Committee of Publishers and Associations.)*

You may order this or any other Oxford University Press publication
by visiting the Oxford University Press website at www.oup.com

To My Husband Chris

Your love and support

are my motivation and inspiration

To My Sons, Michael, Nick and Chris

-and-

In memory of my son, Jimmy

Table of Contents

CHAPTER 3:
THE ADOPTION PROCESS

CHAPTER 4:
THE COSTS OF ADOPTION AND AVAILABLE RESOURCES

CHAPTER 5:
CONSENT TO ADOPTION AND TERMINATION
OF PARENTAL RIGHTS

CHAPTER 6:
POST-ADOPTION CONSIDERATIONS

ABOUT THE AUTHOR

MARGARET C. JASPER is an attorney engaged in the general practice of law in South Salem, New York, concentrating in the areas of personal injury and entertainment law. Ms. Jasper holds a Juris Doctor degree from Pace University School of Law, White Plains, New York, is a member of the New York and Connecticut bars, and is certified to practice before the United States District Courts for the Southern and Eastern Districts of New York, the United States Court of Appeals for the Second Circuit, and the United States Supreme Court.

Ms. Jasper has been appointed to the law guardian panel for the Family Court of the State of New York, is a member of a number of professional organizations and associations, and is a New York State licensed real estate broker operating as Jasper Real Estate, in South Salem, New York.

Margaret Jasper maintains a website at http://www.JasperLawOffice.com.

In 2004, Ms. Jasper successfully argued a case before the New York Court of Appeals, which gives mothers of babies who are stillborn due to medical negligence, the right to bring a legal action and recover emotional distress damages. This successful appeal overturned a 26-year old New York case precedent, which previously prevented mothers of stillborn babies from suing their negligent medical providers.

Ms. Jasper is the author and general editor of the following legal Almanacs:

AIDS Law

The Americans with Disabilities Act

Animal Rights Law

Auto Leasing

Bankruptcy Law for the Individual Debtor

Banks and their Customers

Becoming a Citizen

Buying and Selling Your Home

Commercial Law

Consumer Rights and the Law

Co-ops and Condominiums: Your Rights and Obligations As Owner

Copyright Law

Credit Cards and the Law

Custodial Rights

Dealing with Debt

Dictionary of Selected Legal Terms

Drunk Driving Law

DWI, DUI and the Law

Education Law

Elder Law

Employee Rights in the Workplace

Employment Discrimination Under Title VII

Environmental Law

Estate Planning

Everyday Legal Forms

Executors and Personal Representatives: Rights and Responsibilities

Guardianship and the Law

Harassment in the Workplace

Health Care and Your Rights

Health Care Directives

Hiring Household Help and Contractors: Your Rights and Obligations Under the Law

Home Mortgage Law Primer

Hospital Liability Law

How To Change Your Name

How To Form an LLC

How To Protect Your Challenged Child

How To Start Your Own Business

Identity Theft and How To Protect Yourself

Individual Bankruptcy and Restructuring

Injured on the Job: Employee Rights, Worker's Compensation and Disability Insurance Law

International Adoption

Juvenile Justice and Children's Law

Labor Law

Landlord-Tenant Law

Law for the Small Business Owner

The Law of Adoption

The Law of Attachment and Garnishment

The Law of Buying and Selling

The Law of Capital Punishment

The Law of Child Custody

The Law of Contracts

The Law of Debt Collection

The Law of Dispute Resolution

The Law of Immigration

The Law of Libel and Slander

The Law of Medical Malpractice

The Law of No-Fault Insurance

The Law of Obscenity and Pornography

The Law of Personal Injury

The Law of Premises Liability

The Law of Product Liability

The Law of Speech and the First Amendment

Lemon Laws

Living Together: Practical Legal Issues

Marriage and Divorce

Missing and Exploited Children: How to Protect Your Child

Motor Vehicle Law

Nursing Home Negligence

Patent Law

Pet Law

Prescription Drugs

Privacy and the Internet: Your Rights and Expectations Under the Law

Probate Law

Protecting Your Business: Disaster Preparation and the Law

Real Estate Law for the Homeowner and Broker

Religion and the Law

Retirement Planning

The Right to Die

Rights of Single Parents

Small Claims Court

Social Security Law

Special Education Law

Teenagers and Substance Abuse

Trademark Law

Trouble Next Door: What to do With Your Neighbor

Victim's Rights Law

Violence Against Women

Welfare: Your Rights and the Law

What if It Happened to You: Violent Crimes and Victims' Rights

What if the Product Doesn't Work: Warranties & Guarantees

Workers' Compensation Law

Your Child's Legal Rights: An Overview

Your Rights in a Class Action Suit

Your Rights as a Tenant

Your Rights Under the Family and Medical Leave Act

You've Been Fired: Your Rights and Remedies

INTRODUCTION

According to the National Adoption Clearinghouse, more than 120,000 children are adopted in the United States each year. This Almanac sets forth the various types and circumstances of adoption, the adoption process, and the state and federal laws governing adoption. Consent requirements, termination of parental rights, and the rights of putative fathers are also examined.

This almanac discusses the costs and tax benefits of adoption, and the availability of adoption assistance for special needs children. Post-adoption considerations, such as access to birth records and inheritance issues are discussed along with an overview of international adoption.

The Appendices provides applicable statutes, resource directories, and other pertinent information and data. The Glossary contains definitions of many of the terms used throughout the Almanac.

CHAPTER 1:
AN OVERVIEW OF ADOPTION

WHAT IS ADOPTION?

Adoption is defined as a court action in which an adult assumes legal and other responsibilities for another person, usually a minor. Adoptions occur for a number of reasons. For example, the birth parents may want the child to have a better life than they can provide. A young woman may be faced with an unplanned and unwanted pregnancy and the inability to raise a child. Some adoptive parents are relatives, or step-parents. Foster parents may also choose to adopt their foster children. In order for an adoption to take place, a person available to be adopted must be placed in the home of a person or persons eligible to adopt.

Adoptions are subject to state law. All states and the District of Columbia have laws that specify which persons are eligible as adopting parents, which persons can be adopted, and which persons or entities have the authority to make adoptive placements.

A table of state adoption statutes is set forth in Appendix 1 and a table of state adoption information websites is set forth in Appendix 2.

THE UNIFORM ADOPTION ACT

The Uniform Adoption Act (UAA) was adopted by the National Conference of Commissioners on Uniform State Laws (NCCUSL) in 1994, following five years of intensive discussions with the entire adoption field. The 1994 UAA is the third uniform act NCCUSL has developed and is intended to be a comprehensive statute addressing all areas of adoption law. The current UAA came about because there was a perceived need for uniformity among the states on adoption matters. The UAA, like all model acts, can be introduced and passed in whole or in part by the state legislatures, although to date it has not yet been adopted, in whole, by any state.

The text of the Uniform Adoption Act is set forth in Appendix 3.

WHO MAY ADOPT?

In general any single adult, or a husband and wife jointly, may be eligible to adopt. In some states, married persons may adopt singly if they are legally separated from their spouse or if their spouse is legally incompetent. In addition, a stepparent can adopt the birth child of his or her spouse. A stepparent can usually adopt a stepchild without the birth parent spouse joining in the adoption petition, provided the spouse consents to the adoption.

Eligibility by Age

State statutes dictate the age at which an individual is eligible to adopt. In approximately six states, including Kentucky, Louisiana, Montana, New Jersey, Tennessee, and Washington, prospective parents must be 18 years of age to be eligible to adopt. In three states, Colorado, Delaware, and Oklahoma, the eligibility age is 21; and Georgia and Idaho specify age 25.

A few states allow minors to adopt under certain circumstances, such as when the minor is the spouse of an adult adoptive parent. In approximately six states, including California, Georgia, Nevada, New Jersey, South Dakota, and Utah, the adoptive parents must be at least 10 years older than the person to be adopted and, in Idaho, the adoptive parent must be at least 15 years older.

Eligibility by Residency

Approximately 17 states, including Arizona, Delaware, Georgia, Idaho, Illinois, Indiana, Kentucky, Minnesota, Mississippi, New Mexico, Oregon, Rhode Island, South Carolina, Tennessee, Virginia, Wisconsin,and Wyoming, require that petitioners for adoption be state residents.

The required period of residency ranges from 60 days to 1 year. There are exceptions to the residency requirement in some states. For example, in South Carolina and Indiana, a nonresident can adopt a child with special needs; and in Illinois, Mississippi, New Mexico, and Rhode Island, a nonresident may adopt through an agency.

Sexual Orientation of the Adoptive Parent

The statutory laws in most states are largely silent on the issue of adoption by gay and lesbian persons. At this time, only two states, Florida and Mississippi, explicitly prohibit adoption by homosexuals in their statutes. Utah bars adoption by persons who are cohabiting but not legally married, thus this language could be interpreted to encompass gay and lesbian adoptions. In Connecticut, the sexual orientation of the prospective adoptive parent may be considered, notwithstanding provisions in the state's laws prohibiting discrimination based on sexual orientation.

WHO MAY BE ADOPTED?

All states and the District of Columbia permit the adoption of a child. Some states also allow the adoption of an adult, under certain circumstances. As set forth below, some state statutes specify age, residency, and other requirements for the person to be adopted.

Adoption of a Child

In three states, Colorado, Indiana and Rhode Island, the child to be adopted must be under the age of 18. In five states, Connecticut, Delaware, Montana, Texas, and Wisconsin, the child must be legally free for adoption.

In six states, Arizona, Colorado, South Carolina, Texas, Wisconsin and Wyoming, the child to be adopted must be present in the state at the time the adoption petition is filed. Iowa requires that the child must have resided for a minimum period of 180 days in the home of the prospective adoptive parent.

Adoption of an Adult

The majority of states and the District of Columbia allow the adoption of any person, regardless of their age, including Alaska, Arkansas, Florida, Georgia, Hawaii, Indiana, Kansas, Maine, Massachusetts, Michigan, Minnesota, Mississippi, Montana, Nebraska, New Hampshire, New York, North Carolina, North Dakota, Oklahoma, Oregon, Pennsylvania, Tennessee, Utah, Vermont, Washington, and Wyoming.

Colorado and Rhode Island allow parties to petition the court for the adoption of persons over age 18 but under age 21. Nevada specifies that the adult to be adopted must be younger than the adoptive parent, and West Virginia's statute states that the adopting parent must be a resident of that state to adopt an adult.

Alabama restricts adoption of adults to persons who are permanently and totally disabled or mentally retarded. Ohio allows adoption of an adult only when the person is permanently disabled, mentally retarded, or a stepchild or foster child with whom the relationship was established while the child was a minor.

Idaho, Illinois, and South Dakota require that the adopting parent be in a sustained parental relationship for a specified period of time, ranging from 6 months to 2 years, with the adult to be adopted. Virginia allows the adoption of an adult stepchild, niece, or nephew, as long as the adopted person resided in the home for at least 3 months prior to reaching adulthood, and is at least 15 years younger than the adopting parent.

WHO MAY PLACE A CHILD FOR ADOPTION?

All states and the District of Columbia specifically designate which persons or entities hold the authority to make adoptive placements. In general, any person or entity that has the right to make decisions about a child's care and custody may place that child for adoption.

Agency and Department Placement

Legal entities permitted to place a child for adoption include the state Department of Social Services or licensed child placement agencies. Approximately four states, including Delaware, Indiana, Ohio, and West Virginia, require that *all* adoptive placements be made by the state Department of Social Services or a child placement agency that is licensed by the state.

Non-Agency Placement

Most states allow "non-agency" placement of children for adoption, often referred to as "private" or "independent" adoption. One type of private adoption allowed in most states is the direct placement of a child by the birth parent with an adoptive family. Many states that allow direct placement have detailed statutory regulations in order to protect the interests of the parties to the adoption.

In Florida, Kentucky, Massachusetts, Minnesota, New Mexico, and Rhode Island, parents who wish to make a private placement adoption must notify the state's Department of Social Services, or obtain court approval. An exception to this requirement may be made when the child is being placed with a birth relative.

A few states permit the use of intermediaries in arranging a private placement adoption. These intermediaries are usually attorneys, and their activities, as well as the compensation they are allowed to accept, are strictly regulated, as further discussed in Chapter 2, Types of Adoption, of this Almanac.

CHAPTER 2:
TYPES OF ADOPTION

AGENCY ADOPTION

Prospective adoptive parents who want to adopt a healthy infant with a similar background from the United States may choose to work with a licensed agency. Licensed private agencies need to meet state standards for licensure and have more oversight to ensure quality services unlike unlicensed agencies and intermediaries who do not have the same state oversight.

Agency waiting times for infant adoptions vary tremendously and can be as long as 2 years or more because there are so few infants available for adoption through agencies in the United States. In addition, agency criteria for prospective adoptive parents are often more restrictive for infant adoptions than for adoptions of older children, again because fewer infants are available. Expenses for domestic infant adoption can range from $5,000 to more than $40,000.

In a licensed agency adoption, the birth parents relinquish their parental rights to the agency. Adoptive families then work with adoption agency professionals toward placement. Prospective parents may not have an opportunity to meet the birth parents face to face.

Social workers in agencies make decisions about the match of a child and prospective adoptive parents. Adoptive parents working with private agencies often have little control over the process of identifying a child. This process varies greatly depending on the agency. Some agencies are faith-based and give preference to families from a particular religious background. Many agencies allow birth parents to choose a prospective adoptive family for their child based on profiles or books that families create to share information. In addition, agencies may give preference to certain types of individuals or couples, e.g., due to marital status.

PRIVATE PLACEMENT ADOPTION

When an adoption is carried out without the involvement of an agency, the adoption is known as a private placement adoption. This method of adoption is often preferred by those who wish to avoid being put on an adoption agency waiting list; however, it is often difficult to locate an infant available for private adoption in the United States.

Independent Adoption

In an independent adoption, attorneys assist families; however, birth parents typically give their consent directly to the adoptive family. The prospective adoptive family interacts directly with the birth parents or their attorney. The infants are usually placed with the adoptive parents directly from the hospital after birth.

Even if the birth mother and adoptive parents locate one another independently, they may still take advantage of services offered by a licensed agency. This is called "identified adoption." The agency's role is to conduct the home study for the adoptive parents and counsel the birth mother and father, if available.

Advertising

Because it is so difficult to locate an infant available for private adoption in the United States, some prospective adoptive parents choose to advertise their desire to adopt. Advertising is highly regulated by the states in an effort to protect the parties, and some states even prohibit advertising to facilitate private placement adoptions.

Advertising is defined as the publication in any public medium–print or electronic–of either an interest in adopting a child or the availability of a specific child for adoption. This includes, but is not limited to newspapers, billboards and flyers, radio and television, and the Internet.

Approximately 26 states limit or regulate the use of advertising in adoption placement, including Alabama, California, Connecticut, Delaware, Florida, Georgia, Idaho, Kansas, Kentucky, Louisiana, Maine, Massachusetts, Montana, Nebraska, Nevada, New Hampshire, North Carolina, North Dakota, Ohio, Oklahoma, Oregon, Texas, Utah, Virginia, Washington, and Wisconsin.

Advertising is specifically permitted by birth parents and prospective adoptive parents in Connecticut. In addition, eight states allow advertisement by various agencies and other entities including Florida, Louisiana, Nebraska, North Carolina, Oklahoma, Oregon, Washington, and Wisconsin. Georgia allows the use of public advertising by agencies only.

Advertising is specifically prohibited in Alabama and Kentucky by any person or entity. Further, in California, Delaware, Idaho, Kansas, Maine, Massachusetts, Montana, Nevada, New Hampshire, North Dakota, Ohio and Texas, advertising is prohibited by anyone other than the State department or a licensed agency. Utah specifically prohibits advertising by attorneys, physicians or other persons. In Virginia, no person or agency may advertise any adoption-related activity that is prohibited by state law, and physicians, attorneys and clergy may not advertise their availability to make adoption-related recommendations.

A table of state statutes governing the use of advertising in private placement adoptions is set forth in Appendix 4.

Intermediaries

In addition to advertising, some prospective adoptive parents choose to engage the services of an intermediary to locate birth parents willing to place their child for adoption. However, this method is also highly regulated by the state, and some states prohibit or limit the use of intermediaries to facilitate private placement adoptions.

An intermediary—also known as an adoption facilitator–is a person or organization that brings together a prospective adoptive parent with a birth mother who wants to place her child for adoption. Approximately 34 states and the District of Columbia have laws that regulate the use of intermediaries. In Delaware and Kansas, the use of intermediaries is strictly prohibited. Five states, including Georgia, Montana, Nevada, New Mexico, and Oregon, restrict the placement of children to licensed agencies only. Further, in Kentucky, Massachusetts, Minnesota, Nebraska, New York and the District of Columbia, the placement of children is restricted to either an agency or a member of the child's birth family. Ohio and Oklahoma limit placement to an agency, family member or attorney.

Twelve states, including Alabama, Colorado, Louisiana, Maryland, Missouri, South Carolina, South Dakota, Tennessee, Texas, Utah, Virginia, and West Virginia, regulate the activities of intermediaries by limiting the compensation they can receive. It is illegal for them to receive any payment for the placement of a child, but they may receive reimbursement for actual medical or legal services rendered.

Eight states permit the use of intermediaries, however, the statutes set forth the activities they are permitted to perform and/or required to offer, as follows:

1. In California, Florida, Michigan, and Washington, intermediaries must provide written information about the adoption process;

2. In California, Michigan, and Pennsylvania, intermediaries must provide the adopting parent with any available background information about the child's birth parent;

3. In New Jersey and Pennsylvania, intermediaries must make sure the adopting parents have completed favorable home studies;

4. In California, Florida, and Pennsylvania, intermediaries must report all fees and expenses paid to the court.

5. In Florida, the law requires the intermediary to obtain all necessary consents, file petitions and affidavits, and serve notices of hearings; and

6. In North Carolina and Vermont, the law explicitly states that a parent or guardian must personally select a prospective adoptive parent, and the role of the intermediary is limited to either assisting the birth parent in evaluating that choice, or assisting a prospective adoptive parent in locating a child who is available for adoption.

A table of state statutes governing the use of intermediaries in private placement adoptions is set forth in Appendix 5.

THE OPEN ADOPTION

The open adoption allows the adoptive parents, and often the adopted child, to interact directly with the birth parents. Communication may include letters, e-mails, telephone calls, or visits. In some cases, it may not be in the child's best interests to maintain an open relationship with his or her birth parents, e.g., if the relationship was violent, contact may be traumatic for the child.

The frequency of contact is negotiated and can range from every few years to several times a month or more. Contact often changes as a child gets older and has more questions about his or her adoption.

It is important to note that even in an open adoption, the legal relationship between a birth parent and child is severed, and the adoptive parents are the legal parents of the adopted child.

If an open adoption is being considered, a post-adoption contact agreement should be negotiated, as further discussed in Chapter 6, Post-Adoption Considerations, of this Almanac.

THE STEPPARENT ADOPTION

Most adoptions in the United States are stepparent adoptions. In a stepparent adoption, a parent's new spouse adopts a child the parent had with a previous partner. In most states, a stepparent adoption is much easier to complete than a non-relative adoption. The process is quite simple, especially if the child's other birth parent consents to the adoption.

The procedure is generally the same as for any adoption, but specific steps are sometimes waived or streamlined. For instance, waiting periods, home studies and even the adoption hearing are sometimes dispensed with in a stepparent adoption.

If the other birth parent cannot be found or if he or she refuses to consent to the adoption, the adoption will not be allowed unless his or her parental rights are terminated. The court may terminate the absent parent's rights under the following circumstances:

1. The absent parent has not exercised any parental rights and termination is appropriate;

2. The other parent has willfully failed to support the child or has abandoned the child for a period of time, e.g., one year; or

3. The absent father does not meet the legal definition of presumed father.

THE RELATIVE ADOPTION

In a relative adoption, also known as a kinship adoption, a member of the child's family wishes to adopt the child. For example, grandparents often adopt their grandchildren if the parents die while the children are minors, or if the parents are unable to take care of the children for other reasons.

In most states, relative adoptions are easier to process than non-relative adoptions. If the adopted child has siblings who are not adopted at the same time, relative adoption procedures usually provide for contact between the siblings after the adoption.

FOSTER CARE ADOPTION

There are many children in foster care waiting for adoptive families. Once a match has been made between a family and child, and the prospective adoptive parents have reviewed and feel comfortable accepting the child's social and background information, the prospective parents and the child begin visiting at the direction of the involved adoption professionals. Pre-placement visits vary depending on the situation and the age of the child. After the successful completion of these visits, the child is placed for adoption and comes to live with the family.

Foster Parent Adoption

Many children in foster care who become available for adoption are adopted by their foster parents. In fact, according to the U.S. Department of Health and Human Services, foster parents are the most important source of adoptive families for children in the child welfare system.

Foster parents were not always preferred candidates for adoptive parenthood as they were viewed more as temporary caregivers than a permanent placement home. In fact, foster parents were discouraged, and often prohibited, from adopting their foster children until 1980, when the Federal Adoption Assistance and Child Welfare Act was passed, which supported and subsidized foster parent adoption.

Many states now require that foster parents be considered as an adoption resource, and receive preference under certain circumstances when a child becomes free for adoption. Foster parent adoption is also the basis for two well-recognized practices in adoption, as set forth below.

Legal Risk Placements

In "legal risk placements," children whose situations indicate that parental rights will likely be terminated are placed with foster parents who are willing to adopt if the child becomes free.

Concurrent Planning

In concurrent planning, a practice supported by the Adoption and Safe Families Act (ASFA), the permanency goal of reunification is supplemented by an alternative goal, e.g., adoption, to ensure that if reunification is not possible, the child has a clearly identified permanency option that can quickly be put in place.

Initial placements are made with foster parents who would consider adoption should reunification become impossible, thus minimizing the number of placements for children. For concurrent planning to work, these foster parents must be able to support both the reunification plan, as well as the plan for adoption.

Benefits of Foster Parent Adoption

Foster parent adoption has been found to benefit both the child and the parents. For example, unlike most other types of adoption, the child and the foster parents have already spent time living as a family before the adoption is initiated.

Thus, adoption provides the child with a continuing, legal relationship with a parent they know and trust, and who is already familiar with the child's special needs. In addition, the child does not suffer disruption in their personal life as they generally remain in the same community and attend the same school following adoption.

Costs of Foster Parent Adoption

When foster parents adopt their foster child, they become the sole decision maker over the child without supervision, however, they also lose the financial and other assistance provided by the agency, and become financially and legally responsible for the child. However, adoption assistance subsidies and other post-adoption services may be available to help with some of these costs.

CHAPTER 3:
THE ADOPTION PROCESS

JURISDICTION AND VENUE

In each state, different courts are designated to hear certain types of cases—i.e., the court has "jurisdiction" over the specific type of case. The adoption process falls under the jurisdiction of a court in the state where the adoption occurs, and the person seeking to adopt a child must file the adoption petition with the appropriate state court.

All 50 states and the District of Columbia specify, by statute, the court that has jurisdiction over adoption cases. The name of the specific court varies depending on the state.

1. In Arkansas, Florida, Illinois, Kentucky, Michigan, Missouri, Oregon, South Dakota, Virginia and West Virginia, adoption cases fall under the jurisdiction of the Circuit Court.

2. In Idaho, Kansas, Montana, Nevada, New Mexico, North Dakota, Oklahoma, and Wyoming, adoption cases fall under the jurisdiction of the District Court.

3. In Alaska, Arizona, California, Georgia, New Jersey, North Carolina, Washington, and the District of Columbia, adoption cases fall under the jurisdiction of the Superior Court.

4. In Alabama, Connecticut, Indiana, Maine, Massachusetts, New Hampshire, Ohio, and Vermont, adoption cases fall under the jurisdiction of the Probate Court.

5. In Delaware, Hawaii, New York, Rhode Island, and South Carolina, adoption cases fall under the jurisdiction of the Family Court.

6. In Colorado, Louisiana, and Minnesota, adoption cases fall under the jurisdiction of the Juvenile Court.

7. Adoption cases fall under the jurisdiction of the Court of Equity in Maryland; the Court of Common Please in Pennsylvania; and the County Court in Nebraska and Wisconsin.

8. In Alabama, California, Georgia, Massachusetts, Nebraska and Utah, adoption cases fall under the jurisdiction of the Juvenile Court if the child to be adopted has previously been placed under that court's supervision.

9. In some states, more than one court may have jurisdiction over adoption cases, and either court may hear the adoption petition. For example, in New York, either the family court or probate court has jurisdiction and, in Iowa, either the juvenile or district court has jurisdiction over adoption cases. In Tennessee, either the chancery or circuit court has jurisdiction and, in Texas, a district court or juvenile court may entertain an adoption petition.

Venue refers to the geographic "location" of the court that will hear the adoption petition. In most states, a court having jurisdiction over adoption cases, as set forth above, is located in each county or district, for the convenience of the parties involved in the case. The person seeking to adopt a child will file the adoption petition in the appropriate court in the proper venue. In most cases, the venue will be in the county or district where the person seeking to adopt and/or the adoptive child reside.

A table of state statutes governing court jurisdiction and venue for adoption proceedings is set forth in Appendix 6.

THE HOME STUDY

As part of the adoption process, all states and the District of Columbia require all prospective adoptive parents to participate in a home study.

Purpose of the Home Study

The purpose of the home study is to (1) educate and prepare the adoptive family for adoption; (2) gather information about the prospective parents that will help a social worker match the family with a child whose needs they can meet; and (3) evaluate the fitness of the adoptive family.

Elements of the Home Study Process

In general, to determine suitability of an adoptive placement, the home study looks at the petitioner's physical health, emotional maturity, financial situation, and family and social background. Specific home study processes vary from agency to agency, and from state to state; however, the following elements are generally included in most home studies.

Training Sessions

Many agencies require training sessions for prospective adoptive parents prior to or during the home study process in order to help them better understand the needs of the children waiting for families, and help families decide what type of child they could parent most effectively.

Interviews

There are generally several interview sessions with a social worker in order to ensure an appropriate child placement. Both parents may be interviewed together and separately. The children in the prospective adoptive family will also be included in the home study in some way, and older children may be invited to participate in age appropriate groups during one or more of the sessions.

Home Visit

The home visit is conducted to ensure the adoptive home meets state licensing standards. Some states require an inspection from the local health and fire departments in addition to the visit by the social worker. The agency will generally require the worker to see all areas of the home, including the sleeping arrangements for the child.

Health Statement

Most agencies require prospective adoptive parents to have some form of physical examination. Some agencies have specific requirements. For example, agencies that only place infants with infertile couples may require a physician to confirm the infertility. Other agencies just want to know the prospective parents are essentially healthy, have a normal life expectancy, and are physically and mentally able to handle the care of a child.

If you have a medical condition that is under control, you may still be approved as an adoptive family; however, a serious health problem that affects life expectancy may prevent approval. In addition, if your family has sought counseling or treatment for a mental health condition in the past, you may be asked to provide reports from those visits.

Autobiographical Statement

Many adoption agencies ask prospective adoptive parents to write an autobiographical statement. This statement helps the social worker better understand the family and assists the worker in writing the home study report.

References

Most agencies request contact information for references. The references you list should be individuals who have known you for several years, who have observed you in many situations, and who have visited your home and know of your interest in and involvement with children. Most agencies do not permit relatives to serve as references.

Approval would rarely be denied on the grounds of one negative reference alone. However, if it were one of several negative factors, or if several of the references were negative, the agency might be unable to approve the adoption.

The Background Check

All states and the District of Columbia require that the child placement agency conduct a background investigation to determine the suitability of the prospective adoptive home. While the vast majority of prospective adoptive parents have no criminal or child abuse history, it is important for children's safety to identify those few families who might put children at risk. Public and private agencies need to comply with federal and state laws and policies regarding how the findings of background checks affect eligibility for adoptive parents.

Criminal Record Check

In most states, the background investigation includes a criminal record check of the prospective adoptive parents and all adults residing in the prospective adoptive households. A criminal record check refers specifically to a check of the individual's name in state, local, or Federal law enforcement records for any history of criminal convictions. Many states also require a child abuse and neglect registry check.

The requirement for the type of background check and the individuals who must be included in the check may be found in a statute or regulation, as follows:

1. State or local criminal record checks of the adoptive parent applicant are required in 50 states and the District of Columbia.

2. Federal criminal record checks are required in 24 states including Alabama, Alaska, Arizona, Arkansas, California, Connecticut, Delaware, Florida, Illinois, Indiana, Kentucky, Louisiana, Maine, Michigan, Minnesota, Nebraska, Nevada, New Jersey, New Mexico, North Carolina, Oklahoma, Rhode Island, Vermont, and Washington.

3. Fingerprinting and name-based checks are required as part of the criminal record check in 23 states including Alabama, Arizona, Arkansas, California, Delaware, Florida, Illinois, Indiana, Kentucky, Louisiana, Maine, Maryland, Minnesota, Nevada, New Jersey, New Mexico, New York, Ohio, Oklahoma, Rhode Island, Vermont, Washington, and West Virginia.

4. Child abuse and neglect record checks are required in the District of Columbia and 34 states including Alaska, Arizona, Arkansas, Connecticut, Delaware, Florida, Indiana, Iowa, Kansas, Kentucky, Louisiana, Maine, Maryland, Michigan, Minnesota, Mississippi, Montana, Nebraska, Nevada, New Hampshire, New Jersey, New Mexico, New York, North Carolina, Oklahoma, Pennsylvania, South Carolina, South Dakota, Texas, Utah, Virginia, Washington, West Virginia, and Wisconsin. In Wyoming, the court may order a central registry check as part of the home study.

5. Alaska and Oklahoma require checks of the state sex offender registries.

6. Criminal record checks are required for all adult members of the prospective adoptive parent's household in the District of Columbia and approximately 18 states including Alabama, Alaska, Arizona, Florida, Illinois, Iowa, Kentucky, Louisiana, Maryland, Nevada, New Jersey, New Mexico, North Carolina, Ohio, Oklahoma, Oregon, Utah, and West Virginia.

7. Criminal record checks are required for all adults and older children in the prospective adoptive parents' household in 7 states. Arkansas and Connecticut require checks of all persons over age 16; Massachusetts and Texas require checks of all persons over age 14; Minnesota requires checks for all persons over age 13; and Idaho and Montana require checks for all persons in the household regardless of age.

The information contained in criminal background histories and child abuse reports is incorporated into the adoption home study that is used to help determine whether the adoptive parents' home will be a safe and appropriate placement for a child.

Disqualifying Crimes

If a check reveals that the prospective parent has been convicted of a crime that would raise concerns about that person's ability to safely parent a child, an unfavorable home study may be issued and the adoption petition denied. For example, a state may deny approval of an adoption application if any adult in the household has been convicted of a crime such as sexual abuse of a minor. The types of crimes that would disqualify a prospective adoptive parent are specified in statute or regulation.

In Colorado, Delaware, Florida, Iowa, Kansas, Kentucky, Louisiana, Maryland, Nevada, New Mexico, New York, Oklahoma, Oregon, Utah, Virginia, and the District of Columbia, the list of offenses generally corresponds to those contained in The Adoption and Safe Families Act of 1997 (ASFSA), which is found in title IV-E of the Social Security Act, as discussed below.

In Alabama, Alaska, Arizona, Arkansas, Connecticut, Idaho, Louisiana, Massachusetts, New Jersey, North Carolina, Ohio, Rhode Island, Texas, Virginia, West Virginia, and Wisconsin, the list of offenses is more extensive and may include such crimes as arson, kidnapping, illegal use of weapons or explosives, fraud, forgery, or property crimes such as burglary and robbery.

Delaware, Florida, Kentucky, Nevada, New York, Washington, and the District of Columbia allow approval of an adoptive parent when 5 years have elapsed since being convicted of physical assault, battery or a drug-related offense. A few other states have provisions for approval that require evidence of rehabilitation and/or set longer time limits.

A table of state statutes concerning criminal background checks for prospective adoptive parents is set forth at Appendix 7.

Federal Legislation

State statutes requiring criminal background checks are supported by Federal legislation, as discussed below.

The Adoption and Safe Families Act of 1997 (ASFSA)

The Adoption and Safe Families Act of 1997 (ASFSA), which is found in title IV-E of the Social Security Act, requires criminal record checks for any prospective adoptive parent when adoption assistance payments are to be made under title IV-E.

Under the ASFSA, approval of the adoptive home may not be granted if either of the following is found:

1. The applicant has been convicted of felony child abuse or neglect; spousal abuse; a crime against children, including child pornography; or a crime involving violence, including rape, sexual assault, or homicide.

2. The applicant has been convicted of a felony for physical assault, battery, or a drug-related offense with the past 5 years.

The Child Abuse Prevention and Treatment Act (CAPTA)

In addition to the provisions set forth in the ASFA, the Child Abuse Prevention and Treatment Act (CAPTA) requires that every state conduct a criminal background check for all adults residing in a prospective adoptive home.

The Adam Walsh Child Protection and Safety Act of 2006

Under the Adam Walsh Child Protection and Safety Act, national, fingerprint-based checks as well as child abuse registry checks are required for all adoptive placements.

The Home Study Report

The information gathered from this investigation is known as the home study report, also known as a pre-placement report. In some states, the home study or pre-placement report also includes the following information concerning the prospective adoptive parents:

1. Employment history (Michigan, Montana, New Mexico, New York, North Carolina, Oklahoma, Rhode Island, South Dakota, West Virginia, and Puerto Rico);

2. Racial and ethnic background (Michigan, Montana, North Carolina, Pennsylvania, South Dakota, Vermont, and the District of Columbia);

3. Religious background (Arizona, Illinois, Montana, New York, North Carolina, Pennsylvania, Vermont, and the District of Columbia);

4. History of drug or alcohol abuse (Colorado, Michigan, Montana, North Carolina, Rhode Island, and Vermont); and

5. History of domestic violence (Colorado, Michigan, Minnesota, Montana, North Carolina, and Vermont).

Applicants are also required to provide copies of birth certificates, marriage licenses or certificates, and divorce decrees, if applicable.

The home study report concludes with a summary and the social worker's recommendation as to the age range and number of children recommended for adoption by the prospective parents. On average, the home study process takes 3 to 6 months to complete.

The completed home study report is often used to "introduce" the prospective adoptive family to other agencies or adoption exchanges–i.e., services that list children waiting for families–to assist in matching your family with a waiting child. In some cases, the information may also be shared with birth parents or others.

Ask the agency about the confidentiality of the home study report and how extensively your information will be shared. Some agencies allow prospective parents to read the home study report, others do not.

COLLECTION OF FAMILY INFORMATION ABOUT THE ADOPTED CHILD, BIRTH PARENTS AND ADOPTIVE PARENTS

Requirements for collecting information about the parties involved in an adoption vary from state to state. Each state has laws that specify the kinds of information that may be collected and shared among the parties.

Who May Collect Information

State laws specify the persons or entities authorized to collect information. In most states, information about the child to be adopted and the child's birth family is compiled by the child placement agency or the department of social services. In some states, the court may designate another qualified person, such as a social worker or specially trained investigator, to complete the history of the birth family.

In approximately nine states, the child's parent or other person placing the child for adoption is required to submit family information to the court. The states that currently have this requirement include: Arizona, Indiana, Iowa, Montana, North Carolina, Texas, Vermont, Washington, and West Virginia.

As discussed above, information about the adoptive parents is collected as part of the adoption home study or investigation and, in most states, this study is completed by a child placement agency or the department of social services. Other individuals, such as social workers or private investigators, may also be certified to conduct these investigations.

Information About the Adopted Child

Generally, information compiled about the child to be adopted includes:

1. Medical and genetic history;

2. Family and social background;

3. Mental health history;

4. Placement history; and

5. Any history of abuse or neglect.

Some states are more specific in their requirements and include more detailed information on the child, including dental, immunization, and developmental history, as well as any school records.

In addition, Michigan, Missouri, Nevada, Oklahoma, Rhode Island, Texas, and Vermont require information on whether the child is eligible for any State or Federal adoption assistance.

Information About the Birth Parents

Generally, information compiled about the birth parents includes:

1. Medical and genetic history;

2. Family and social background;

3. Mental health history;

4. Religious background;

5. Ethnic and racial background; and

6 Educational level attained.

Some states also collect information concerning physical appearance, talents, hobbies, field of occupation, and drugs taken by the mother during pregnancy.

In most instances, only non-identifying information is shared with the adoptive parents. However, in Colorado and New York, the names, addresses, and other identifying information about the birth parents, if obtainable, will be provided to the adoptive parents.

Information About the Adoptive Parents

As discussed above, prior to or immediately after an adoption petition is filed with the court, an investigation of the prospective adoptive parents is conducted to determine the suitability of the home for the child to be adopted. The information collected is included in the home study report.

THE PLACEMENT PROCESS

Once the home study is completed, the placement process begins. At this time, a specific child is identified for placement with the prospective adoptive parents. Depending on the type of adoption, this process and the potential time involved in waiting for a child varies greatly.

In an independent adoption, an attorney or facilitator may help the adoptive parents identify expectant parents, or the parents may locate them on their own if allowed by state law. If a licensed private adoption agency is being used to pursue a domestic infant adoption, the expectant parents may select a family from among several prospective adoptive families.

In the case of foster care adoption, the prospective adoptive parents may review information about a number of children who are waiting for families. They are often given the opportunity for pre-placement visits to get to know a child before he or she moves into the adoptive home. Also, many foster parents adopt the foster children already living in their homes if the children become available for adoption.

FINALIZING THE ADOPTION

All adoptions need to be finalized in court. Usually a child lives with the adoptive family for at least 6 months before the adoption is finalized legally. During this time, a social worker may visit several times to ensure the child is well cared for and to gather information for the required court reports.

After this period, the agency or attorney will submit a written recommendation of approval of the adoption to the court, and the adoptive parents can file the adoption petition with the court to complete the adoption.

The Adoption Petition

A standard adoption petition will generally include the following information:

1. The names, ages, and residence address of the adoptive parents;

2. The name, age, and legal parentage of the child to be adopted;

3. The relationship between the adoptive parents and the child to be adopted, if any, such as stepparent or relative;

4. The legal reason that the birthparents' rights are being terminated, e.g., voluntary relinquishment;

5. A statement that the adoptive parents are the appropriate people to adopt the child; and

6. A statement that the adoption is in the child's best interests.

The written consents of the birthparents or the court order terminating their parental rights may be filed along with the petition. Adoptive parents also often include a request for an official name change for the child.

Notice

Before the adoption hearing, anyone who is required to consent to the adoption must receive notice, as specified by statute. Usually this includes the biological parents, the adoption agency, the child's legal representative if a court has appointed one, and the child, if he or she is old enough, e.g., 12 to 14 years in most states.

The Adoption Hearing and Order

At the adoption hearing, if the court determines that the adoption is in the child's best interest, the judge will issue an order approving and finalizing the adoption. This order, often called a final decree of adoption, legalizes the new parent-child relationship, and usually changes the child's name to the name the adoptive parents have chosen.

CHAPTER 4:
THE COSTS OF ADOPTION AND AVAILABLE RESOURCES

IN GENERAL

Prospective adoptive parents are understandably concerned about the costs associated with adoption. Costs depend on a number of factors, and can vary from $0 to more than $40,000. Thus, it is prudent to thoroughly investigate the different types of adoption and the costs associated with the services provided. If a particular agency is being considered to handle the adoption, they should be able to provide information about the specific costs,

In general, as further discussed below, the following is a range of adoption costs categorized by the type of adoption:

1. Foster Care Adoption: $0 - $2,500

2. Domestic Infant Adoption Costs: $5,000 - $40,000

3. Licensed Private Agency Adoption: $5,000 - $40,000

4. Independent Adoption: $8,000 - $40,000

5. Facilitated/Unlicensed Adoption: $5,000 - $40,000

6. International Adoption: $7,000 - $30,000

Although the costs may seem prohibitive, in many cases, tax credits, subsidies, employer benefits, and loans or grants can help with adoption costs, as further discussed below.

TYPES OF ADOPTION EXPENSES

As discussed below, adoption expenses basically fall into two categories: (1) universal expenses, i.e. those expenses that occur for every type of adoption; and (2) adoption-specific expenses, i.e., those expenses that are associated with a particular type of adoption. All adoptive parents pay some combination of universal and adoption-specific expenses.

Universal Expenses

Universal expenses are incurred by every person who adopts a child. These expenses include the cost of the home study, and the legal fees and court costs associated with the adoption.

Cost of the Home Study

The cost of the home study depends on what kind of adoption you are pursuing. Agencies conducting domestic adoptions of children from foster care, such as the state Department of Social Services, may not charge a fee for the home study. If these agencies do charge a fee, they often are modest, e.g., $300 to $500. However, once you adopt a child from foster care you can usually obtain reimbursement for this fee.

For domestic infant adoption, international adoption, or independent adoption, a private agency or certified social worker in private practice might charge from $1,000 to $3,000 for the home study. Other services, such as an application fee and pre-placement services, may be included in this fee.

Legal Fees and Court Costs

All domestic adoptions and some international adoptions must be finalized in a court in the United States. All of these procedures incur court costs, and may require representation of an attorney, depending on the jurisdiction. The cost for court document preparation can range from $500 to $2,000, while the cost for legal representation may range from $2,500 to $12,000 or more in some states.

Adoption-Specific Expenses

In addition to the costs common to every adoption, adoptive parents generally incur costs specific to their type of adoption, e.g., domestic infant adoption, foster care adoption, international adoption, etc. These expenses are in addition to the universal expenses described above in most cases.

Foster Care Adoption Costs

Most public agencies in the foster care system place children with special needs only, e.g., older children, minority children, children with disabilities, and children who must be placed with siblings. Up-front fees and expenses may range from $0 to $2,500, including attorney's fees and travel expenses. In foster care adoptions, fees are often kept to a minimum or even waived, so that final costs to parents are negligible.

Domestic Infant Adoption Costs

Domestic infant adoption costs vary widely according to the type of agency used and the individual adoption circumstances, and can range from $5,000 to $40,000. It is important for prospective adoptive parents to fully understand what is included in agency and attorney fees. As set forth below, domestic infant adoptions fall into three general categories.

Licensed Private Agency Adoption Costs

The costs for a licensed private agency adoption include a fee charged by the agency, and may also include the cost of the home study, birth parent counseling, adoptive parent preparation and training, and social work services involved in matching a child to a prospective family. The costs can range from $5,000 to $40,000.

The fees charged by licensed agencies are generally predictable, and some even have sliding fee scales based on family income. In addition, some agencies may offer reduced fees to prospective parents who locate a birth parent on their own but who need the agency for counseling, facilitation, home study, and supervision services.

Independent Adoption Costs

The costs of an independent adoption handled by an attorney generally include medical expenses for the birth mother as well as separate legal fees for representing adoptive and birth parents, and any allowable fees for advertising. Additional medical expenses may be required in situations in which there are birth complications. The costs can range from $8,000 to $40,000.

As discussed below, state laws restrict many of these costs, including any reimbursements to the birth mother. Restrictions may also exist regarding advertisements seeking expectant parents.

Compared to licensed agency adoptions, the costs of independent adoptions may be less predictable. In addition, costs may not be reimbursable in cases in which a birth mother changes her mind and chooses to parent her child.

Facilitated/Unlicensed Adoption Costs

The costs of a facilitated/unlicensed agency adoption are generally the same as costs of licensed agencies. However, in states that allow adoptive placements by facilitators, these placements are largely unregulated. Prospective parents may have no recourse if the adoption does not proceed as expected. The costs can range from $5,000 to $40,000.

International Adoption Costs

The agencies that provide international adoption services charge fees that range from $7,000 to $30,000. These fees generally include dossier and immigration processing, and court costs. In some cases, they may include a required donation to the foreign orphanage or agency. Overall costs may depend on the type of entity in the foreign country that is responsible for placing the child, e.g., government agency, government orphanage, charitable foundation, attorney, and facilitator.

Depending on the country, additional costs may include:

1. Child foster care;

2. Travel and lodging for the prospective parents to process the adoption abroad;

3. Escorting fees, charged when the prospective parents do not travel but instead hire escorts to accompany the child on the flight;

4. Child's medical care and treatment;

5. Translation fees;

6. Foreign attorney fees;

7. Foreign agency fees;

8. Passport fees; and

9. Visa processing fees and the costs of the visa medical examination.

STATE REGULATION OF ADOPTION EXPENSES

In an effort to protect the parties to an adoption, approximately 45 states and the District of Columbia have enacted laws that regulate the fees and expenses adoptive parents are permitted to pay when adopting a child. The fees and expenses that are generally addressed by statute include agency fees; legal fees and costs; and the expenses of the birth mother. In most states, the dollar amount of allowable expenses are generally required to be "reasonable and customary," however, a few states set a specific dollar amount that cannot be exceeded.

Birth Parent Expenses

The types of birth parent expenses commonly allowed by statute include:

1. Maternity-related medical and hospital costs;

2. Temporary living expenses of the mother during pregnancy;

3. Counseling fees;

4. Legal fees and costs;

5. Guardian ad litem fees;

6. Travel, food and lodging expenses when required for court appearances or accessing services;

7. Foster care for the child, when necessary.

Illinois, Kentucky, Michigan, Minnesota, Montana, New Hampshire, North Dakota, and Wisconsin specifically exclude certain expenses, such as educational expenses, vehicles, vacations, permanent housing, or any other payment that represents a monetary gain for the birth parent. Idaho is the only state that requires reimbursement of expenses to the prospective adoptive parents if the birth parent decides not to place the child for adoption.

In addition, a number of states limit the time period during which the birth parent may receive payments for living expenses or psychological counseling, e.g., 30 days to 6 weeks following birth.

Agency Fees and Costs

Most states authorize adoption agencies to collect "reasonable and customary" fees for the adoption services they provide. In Alabama, California, Indiana, Maine, and Wisconsin, the statutes specify a dollar amount for agency fees or specific services the agency provides.

The services that adoption agencies typically provide include preparation of the pre-placement and post-placement home studies of the adoptive family, a social and medical history of the birth family; and birth family counseling. Some agencies receive the payments for the birth parent's expenses and disburse those payments accordingly.

Intermediary Fees

An intermediary—also known as an adoption facilitator—is a person or organization that matches a prospective adoptive parent with a birth mother who would like to place her child for adoption. Many states have enacted laws to restrict or regulate the use of intermediaries in independent adoptions in an effort to ensure that neither the intermediary or a member of the birth family profits form the child's placement.

In some states, the use of intermediaries is prohibited, and all adoptive placements must take place through licensed or state agencies. Some states allow the use of intermediaries but restrict their activities by specifically prohibiting the tender or receipt of any payment for either placing a child or for obtaining a consent to adoption.

In those states where intermediaries are permitted, their fees are limited to "reasonable and customary" compensation for actual services provided.

Reporting Requirements

Approximately 37 states require an accounting of all adoption-related expenses. Typically, the accounting is in the form of a statement or affidavit of expenses, and is made part of the adoption petition that is submitted to the court that has jurisdiction over the proceeding. Some states require the submission of a receipt to document each expense. The court has the discretion to review all adoption-related expenses, and may deny or modify any expense it deems unreasonable, unnecessary or not permitted under the law.

A table of allowable adoption expenses, by state, is set forth in Appendix 8.

ADOPTION ASSISTANCE RESOURCES

There are a number of resources available to prospective adoptive parents, depending on the type of adoption, the child being adopted, and the circumstances under which the adoption takes place.

Adoption Assistance for Special Needs Children

Children with special needs who are adopted from foster care may qualify for adoption assistance, which is paid to adoptive families to help them defray expenses related to their child's need for ongoing therapies or treatments or to cover certain one-time expenses.

Each state has its own definition of children with special needs, but they often include children who are older, have disabilities, belong to a minority group, or must be placed with siblings. To facilitate the adoption of these children, who often are in foster care, States may provide reimbursements for some adoption costs, as well as subsidies for some children.

There are two major funding sources of adoption assistance or subsidies: (1) the Federal Title IV-E program (42 USC 673) under the Social Security Act; and (2) state programs, which vary from state to state.

Adoption subsidy programs are typically categorized by the manner in which they are funded. Under the Federal Adoption Assistance Program, Federal Title IV-E matching funds are given to states that provide adoption assistance payments to parents who adopt children with special needs, as that term is defined by the state. Federal and state adoption subsidies generally help the adoptive parents pay for the ongoing care of children with special physical, mental, or emotional needs. Some children may also qualify for Supplemental Security Income (SSI) or Medicaid coverage.

In addition, the program authorizes Federal matching funds for states that reimburse the nonrecurring adoption expenses of adoptive parents of children with special needs. Nonrecurring expenses include those expenses related to finalizing the adoption, such as home study fees, attorney fees, travel expenses, etc.

Not all children who receive adoption assistance from states are eligible for Federal Title IV-E funds. The non-Title IV-E children's adoption subsidies are paid solely by the state in which their adoption agreement was signed, without any Federal reimbursement.

Adoption subsidies take various forms in different states, and depend on the child's needs and the state agency's program. Six states, including Arkansas, Colorado, Michigan, Mississippi, Montana, and South Carolina, provide subsidies for children in state custody regardless of the residency of the adoptive parents. Families interested in adopting a child with special needs should contact their local department of social services to determine what assistance is available in their state.

Eligibility for Adoption Assistance

The Federal definition under Title IV-E for a child with disabilities has three parts, as set forth under the Title IV-E program (42 USC § 673), whereby the state must determine that all three of the following conditions exist:

1. The child cannot or should not be returned to the home of the parents.

2. There exists, with respect to the child, a specific factor, such as ethnic background, age, or membership in a sibling group that would make placement difficult.

3. Reasonable efforts have been made for unsubsidized placement except where a specific adoptive placement is in the child's best interests. Twelve states provide for specific exceptions to the "reasonable efforts" requirement if the child has formed an attachment

to the foster parent and it is determined that disrupting that attachment would be detrimental to the child. These states include: Alabama, Arizona, Arkansas, California, Connecticut, Florida, Kentucky, Maryland, New Jersey, Oklahoma, South Carolina, and West Virginia.

Federal law does not provide an exhaustive list of special needs conditions and thereby allows the states much discretion in determining the definition of a child with special needs.

Limitation on Adoption Assistance

Although subsidies are available for children with special needs, such subsidies are not unlimited. For example, Federal law does not allow the financial status of the adoptive parents to be a factor in determining the child's eligibility under Title IV-E. However, state agencies consider the parents' circumstances and the needs of the child when establishing the subsidy amount under the Federal program.

Moreover, under Title IV-E, adoption assistance may not exceed the amount that is allowable under foster family care or the reasonable fees for services in cases where special services are required.

For state-funded subsidies, some states have financial means tests that determine the amount a prospective adoptive family may receive under state funding. Georgia, Kansas, Louisiana, Maine, Massachusetts, Minnesota, New Hampshire, and Washington require agencies to consider the parents' income when determining subsidy amounts.

For both federally funded and state-funded subsidies, agreements must be negotiated before the adoption is finalized. However, adoptive families may request adoption assistance after the adoption is finalized, and such requests may be approved under specific conditions, based on the funding source.

For state-funded subsidies, some states permit funding for requests made after finalization, provided that state-specific criteria are met. Federal Title IV-E funds may be available for monthly subsidy only for those children who meet Title IV-E eligibility criteria prior to finalization.

However, at any point after finalization, adoptive parents may request a fair hearing, and assistance may be approved if one of the following situations has occurred:

1. The state agency failed to notify parents of the availability of assistance;

2. Assistance was denied based on an erroneous determination that the child did not meet special needs criteria;

3. Relevant facts, which may have affected the special needs determination, were known but not presented to the adoptive parents prior to finalization;

4. A condition existed but was not discovered prior to finalization.

Termination or Modification of Adoption Assistance

Under Title IV-E, adoption assistance payments may continue until the child is age 18, or at the option of the state, until the child is age 21 if the child has a physical or mental disability that warrants continued assistance. Payments also terminate if the state determines that the parents are no longer legally responsible for the support of the child, or if the child is no longer receiving any support from the parents.

For an exclusively state-funded subsidy, each individual state determines when the subsidy shall terminate. Payments may be readjusted according to the changing needs of the child and the adoptive family.

In addition, some states provide separate subsidies for special services, such as extraordinary medical treatment or other services needed by the child that regular programs like Medicaid do not cover. For example, Connecticut, Louisiana, Michigan, and Washington provide separate subsidy payments for medical treatments or hospitalization, and Illinois, Maryland, and New Hampshire offer special purpose grants for extraordinary expenses that maintenance subsidies are unable to cover.

In addition, Federal law requires that states afford the right to appeal and a fair hearing before the appropriate state agency to any individual whose claim for benefits is denied.

The states determine how frequently the parents must be reevaluated for continued subsidies received from both Federal and state sources. Most states evaluate adoptive parents annually to determine whether the need for continued assistance exists; however, some states evaluate such parents more or less frequently than once a year.

Employer Benefits

Many employers provide a range of benefits for families who adopt. Adoption benefits fall into three general categories: (1) information resources; (2) financial assistance; and (3) parental leave policies.

Information Resources

Information resources made available to employees may include referrals to licensed adoption agencies, support groups, and organizations;

access to an adoption specialist to answer questions about the process; and help with special situations, such as a special needs adoption. Many employers that offer this type of benefit contract with a human resources consulting firm to provide these services to employees.

Financial Assistance

Financial benefits take different forms. Some employers provide a lump sum payment for an adoption, usually between $1,000 and $15,000. Other employers pay certain fees related to an adoption. Still others partially reimburse employees for expenses.

Typical reimbursement plans cover 80 percent of certain itemized expenses up to an established ceiling. Some employers reimburse at a higher rate for adoptions of children with special needs.

Most frequently, employer-provided financial assistance covers public or private agency fees, court costs, and legal fees. Employers also might help with foreign adoption fees, medical costs, temporary foster care charges, transportation costs, pregnancy costs for a birth mother, and counseling fees associated with placement and transition.

Some employers pay benefits per adoption, while others pay per child adopted. In most cases, the benefits are paid after the adoption is finalized, although some employers may pay benefits when the child is placed or as the expenses are incurred.

Parental Leave

In many cases, employers are required to grant parental leave to parents who have adopted a child. Under the federal Family Medical and Leave Act (FMLA) employers with 50 or more employees are required to offer both mothers and fathers up to 12 weeks of unpaid leave upon the birth or adoption of a child. The law ensures that employees can return to their current jobs or an equivalent position, and it requires employers to continue the employee's health benefits during the leave period.

Some employers allow employees to take more than the required 12 weeks of unpaid leave. In addition, employees may be permitted to combine accumulated paid leave (such as vacation or sick leave) with unpaid leave to extend their total leave. Some employers even offer paid leave for employees who adopt a child. Certain employers may be bound by public and private union contracts that have provisions for adoption leave.

Eligibility and Conditions

Eligibility for adoption benefits usually depends on employment status, e.g., full-time employees. Employers also might base eligibility on length of employment or participation in a company-sponsored health plan.

The type of adoption also can affect the benefits offered. For example, some employers do not provide benefits when a stepparent adopts his or her stepchild or stepchildren. Some employers specify that the child being adopted cannot be older than 16 or 18 years. Others offer enhanced benefits for the adoption of a child with special needs.

For more information, the reader is advised to contact the human resources department of their employer, who can provide them with information about available benefits.

Loans and Grants

Adoptive parents may be eligible to receive a loan or grant to offset some of their adoption costs. Such programs may have specific requirements regarding the type of adoption that is eligible, or they may give preference to families with the greatest financial need or with other specific characteristics. Many agencies also have adoption grant programs.

Tax Credits

Adoption tax credits may be available to defray some adoption costs. The amount may depend on family income and any other adoption benefits. Parents may want to check with a tax professional to determine applicable benefits.

Federal Adoption Tax Credits

For all types of adoption, a Federal adoption tax credit of up to $10,960 is available for qualifying expenses paid to adopt an eligible child, including a child with special needs. The adoption credit is an amount subtracted from the taxpayer's tax liability. Although the credit is generally allowed for the year following the year in which the expenses are paid, a taxpayer who paid qualifying expenses in the current year for an adoption which became final in the current year, may be eligible to claim the credit on the current year return.

The adoption credit is not available for any reimbursed expense. In addition to the credit, certain amounts reimbursed by your employer for qualifying adoption expenses may be excludable from your gross income.

For both the credit and the exclusion, qualifying expenses include:

1. Reasonable and necessary adoption fees;

2. Court costs;

3. Attorney fees;

4. Traveling expenses, including amounts spent for meals and lodging while away from home; and

5. Other expenses directly related to and for which the principal purpose is the legal adoption of an eligible child.

An eligible child must be under 18 years old, or be physically or mentally incapable of caring for himself or herself. The adoption credit or exclusion cannot be taken for a child who is not a United States citizen or resident unless the adoption becomes final.

An eligible child is also a child with special needs if he or she is a United States citizen or resident, and a state determines that the child cannot or should not be returned to his or her parent's home and probably will not be adopted unless assistance is provided. Under certain circumstances, the amount of your qualified adoption expenses may be increased if you adopted an eligible child with special needs.

The credit and exclusion for qualifying adoption expenses are each subject to a dollar limit and an income limit. Under the dollar limit the amount of the adoption credit or exclusion is limited to the dollar limit for that year for each effort to adopt an eligible child. If you can take both a credit and an exclusion, this dollar amount applies separately to each. The dollar limit for a particular year must be reduced by the amount of qualifying expenses taken into account in previous years for the same adoption effort.

The income limit on the adoption credit or exclusion is based on the taxpayer's modified adjusted gross income. If the modified AGI is below the beginning phase out amount for the year, the income limit will not affect the credit or exclusion. If the modified AGI is more than the beginning phase out amount for the year, the credit or exclusion will be reduced. If the modified AGI is above the maximum phase out amount for the year, the credit or exclusion will be eliminated.

Generally, if the adoptive parents are married, they must file a joint return to take the adoption credit or exclusion. If the adoptive parents' filing status is married filing separately, the taxpayer can take the credit or exclusion only if he or she meets special requirements.

To take the credit or exclusion, the taxpayer must complete IRS Form 8839 (Qualified Adoption Expenses) and attach the form to the taxpayer's IRS Form 1040 or 1040A.

IRS Form 8839 (Qualified Adoption Expenses) is set forth in Appendix 9.

Prospective adoptive parents can find information about tax rules regarding adoption at the IRS website (http://www. irs.ustreas.gov).

State Tax Credits

Several states have enacted state tax credits for families adopting children from the public child welfare system in that state. Some are restricted to adoptions from foster care, while others are not.

Adoption Taxpayer Identification Number

An Adoption Taxpayer Identification Number (ATIN) is issued by the Internal Revenue Service as a temporary taxpayer identification number for the child in a domestic adoption when the adopting taxpayers do not have and/or are unable to obtain the child's social security number (SSN).

Taxpayers need an ATIN if they are in the process of adopting a child and are able to claim the child as their dependent or are able to claim a child care credit. Recent tax law changes require that when a taxpayer lists a person's name on their federal income tax return, they must provide a valid identifying number for that person. The ATIN is to be used by the adoptive parent taxpayers on their federal income tax return to identify the child while final domestic adoption is pending.

As soon as the adoption becomes final, the adopting parents should obtain a social security number for the child and notify the Internal Revenue Service of the new number. The IRS will then deactivate the ATIN.

CHAPTER 5:
CONSENT TO ADOPTION AND
TERMINATION OF PARENTAL RIGHTS

REQUIREMENT OF CONSENT

Consent refers to the agreement by a parent, or a person or agency acting in place of a parent, to relinquish a child for adoption and release all rights and duties with respect to that child. Consent to adoption is regulated by state statutes, not by Federal laws, and states differ in the way they regulate consent. In most states, the consent must be in writing and either witnessed and notarized or executed before a judge or other designated official.

State legislatures have developed a range of provisions designed to ensure protection for all individuals involved in the adoption, including: (1) the children—to prevent unnecessary and traumatic separations from their adult caregivers; (2) the birth parents—to prevent uninformed, hurried, or coerced decisions; and (3) the adoptive parents—to prevent anxiety about the legality of the adoption process.

A table of state statutes governing consent in adoption proceedings is set forth in Appendix 10.

Right to Consent

Birth Parents

In all states, the birth mother and the birth father—if he has properly established paternity—hold the primary right of consent to adoption of their child. In those states where there is a putative father registry, an unwed birth father who fails to register in the prescribed manner and within the proper time period may lose the right to consent. Other jurisdictions require an unwed father to file a notice of his paternity claim within a certain period of time and, if he fails to do so, his consent to adoption may not be required. In addition, an unwed father's consent may not be required if he fails to respond to notice of the adoption proceeding.

As set forth below, a court may terminate the rights of one or both parents for a variety of reasons, including: abandonment; failure to support the child; mental incompetence; or a finding of parental unfitness due to abuse or neglect. In that case, the court may determine that consent of the birth parents is not needed.

Other Person or Legal Entity

When neither birth parent is available to give consent, the responsibility can fall to another person legal entity, such as:

1. An agency that has custody of the child;

2. Any person who has been given custody;

3. A guardian or guardian ad litem;

4. The court having jurisdiction over the child;

5. A close relative of the child; or

6. A "next friend" of the child, who is a responsible adult appointed by the court.

Consent of the Child

Nearly all states and the District of Columbia require that older children give consent to their adoption. Colorado requires that the child be provided with counseling prior to giving consent.

Approximately 25 states and the District of Columbia set the age of consent at 14, including: Alabama, Delaware, Georgia, Illinois, Indiana, Iowa, Kansas, Maine, Michigan, Minnesota, Mississippi, Missouri, Nebraska, Nevada, New Hampshire, New Mexico, New York, Oregon, Rhode Island, South Carolina, Tennessee, Vermont, Virginia, Washington, and Wyoming.

Eighteen states require a child's consent at age 12, including: Arizona, California, Colorado, Connecticut, Florida, Idaho, Kentucky, Massachusetts, Montana, North Carolina, Ohio, Oklahoma, Pennsylvania, South Dakota, Texas, Utah, West Virginia and Wisconsin.

Six states require a child's consent at age 10, including: Alaska, Arkansas, Hawaii, Maryland, New Jersey and North Dakota.

Louisiana does not currently address the issue of consent by a minor adoptive child in its statute.

In 11 states, the child's consent may not be required if it is determined that the child lacks the mental capacity to consent. These states include: Alabama, Idaho, Illinois, Kansas, Missouri, Montana, New Jersey, New Mexico, South Carolina, Tennessee, and Utah.

In 16 states, in its discretion, the court may not require the child's consent if it is in the best interest of the child. These states include: Alaska, Arkansas, Delaware, Florida, Hawaii, Kentucky, New Hampshire, New York, North Carolina, Ohio, Oklahoma, South Carolina, Texas, Vermont, Virginia, and West Virginia.

Timing of Consent

As set forth below, approximately 47 states and the District of Columbia specify, in statute, when a birth parent may execute consent to adoption. Idaho, New York, and Oregon do not specify any time frame for executing consent.

Sixteen states allow birth parents to consent at any time after the birth of the child, including: Alaska, Arkansas, California, Colorado, Delaware, Georgia, Indiana, Maine, Maryland, Michigan, North Carolina, North Dakota, Oklahoma, South Carolina, Wisconsin, and Wyoming.

Approximately 12 states allow an alleged birth father to execute consent at any time before or after the child's birth, including: Alabama, Delaware, Hawaii, Indiana, Louisiana, Nevada, New Jersey, North Carolina, Oklahoma, Pennsylvania, Texas, and Virginia.

Thirty states and the District of Columbia require a waiting period before consent can be executed. The shortest waiting periods are 12 hours (Kansas) and 24 hours (Utah), and the longest are 10 days (California and Washington) and 15 days (Rhode Island).

The most common waiting period, required in 15 states and the District of Columbia is 72 hours (3 days). Theses states include: Arizona, Illinois, Iowa, Kentucky, Minnesota, Mississippi, Montana, Nevada, New Hampshire, New Jersey, Ohio, Pennsylvania, Tennessee, Virginia, and West Virginia.

Waiting periods in other states vary: Vermont (36 hours); (Connecticut, Florida, Missouri, Nebraska, New Mexico, Texas, and Washington (48 hours); Massachusetts (4th day after child's birth); Louisiana and South Dakota (5 days); California (after birth mother's discharge from hospital following birth).

Two states—Alabama and Hawaii—allow the mother to consent before the birth of the child; however, the decision to consent must be reaffirmed after the child is born.

Manner of Consent

The manner in which consent can be executed varies considerably from state to state. In many states, including the District of Columbia, consent may be executed by a written statement witnessed and/or notarized before a notary public. Other states may require an appearance before a judge, or the filing of a petition of relinquishment. Some states require that the parent be given certain services prior to giving consent, including: (1) counseling; (2) an explanation of his or her rights and the legal effect of relinquishment; or (3) legal counsel. In cases where custody has previously been placed with an agency, the head of the agency may sign an affidavit of consent.

Minor Birth Parent

In most states, a birth parent who is a minor is treated no differently than other birth parents. However, in some states, the minor parent must be provided with separate counsel prior to the execution of consent, or a guardian ad litem must be appointed to either review or execute the consent. In Kansas, Maryland, Montana, and Vermont, the appointment of separate counsel is required. In Alabama, Arkansas, Connecticut, Kentucky, Michigan, and Rhode Island, the appointment of a guardian ad litem is required. In Louisiana, Michigan, Minnesota, New Hampshire, and Rhode Island, the consent of the minor's parents must be obtained.

Revocation of Consent

Because adoption is designed to create a permanent, stable home for the child, a validly executed relinquishment and consent to adopt is intended to be final and irrevocable. Therefore, the right of a birth parent to revoke his or her consent is strictly limited and, in Massachusetts and Utah, the statutes specifically state that all consents are irrevocable.

In most states, however, the law provides that consent may be revoked prior to the entry of the final adoption decree under certain circumstances, or within specified time limits. The circumstances under which consent may be revoked are set forth below.

Consent Obtained by Fraud, Duress or Coercion

In the following states, if consent to adopt was obtained by fraud, duress or coercion, a claim may be filed for revocation of consent: Alabama, Arizona, Colorado, Florida, Illinois, Kansas, Louisiana, New Hampshire, New Jersey, New Mexico, North Carolina, Oklahoma,

Oregon, Rhode Island, South Carolina, South Dakota, Virginia, Washington, West Virginia, Wisconsin, and Wyoming.

Consent May Be Withdrawn Within Specified Time Period

In the following states, the birth parent is allowed to withdraw consent within a specified period of time, after which consent becomes irrevocable: Arkansas (10 days); California (30 days in a direct placement); Delaware (60 days); Georgia (10 days) Kentucky (20 days); Maryland (30 days); Mississippi (6 months); Missouri (until adoption confirmed by court); Oklahoma (15 days for an extrajudicial consent); Virginia (10 days in a direct placement, 7 days in an agency placement); and the District of Columbia (10 days).

Consent Must be Withdrawn Within Specified Time Period Unless Fraud or Duress

In the following states, the birth parent is allowed to withdrawn consent within a specified period of time, after which consent becomes irrevocable unless there is evidence of fraud or duress: Iowa (96 hours); Maine (3 days); Minnesota (10 days); North Carolina (7 days); Oklahoma (30 days); Pennsylvania (30 days); Tennessee (10 days); Texas (10 days); Vermont (21 days); and Virginia (15 days).

Revocation of Consent in Best Interests of Child

In the following states, the birth parent is allowed to withdrawn consent within a specified period of time, after which consent becomes irrevocable unless it can be shown that revocation is in the best interests of the child: Alaska (10 days); New York (45 days for extrajudicial consents; judicial consents are irrevocable); and Rhode Island (180 days).

Withdrawal of Consent in Best Interests of Child

In the following states, the birth parent may withdraw consent if it is in the best interests of the child: Alabama, Connecticut, Hawaii, Indiana, New Hampshire, North Dakota, Ohio, and South Carolina.

Mutual Agreement of Parties

In the following states, the birth parents and adoptive parents can mutually agree to the withdrawal of consent: Montana, North Carolina, Oklahoma, Vermont, Virginia, and West Virginia.

Prior to Adoption Finalization

In the following states, consent may be withdrawn if the adoptive placement is not finalized with a specific family or within a specified period of time: California (if placement not made within 30 days); Maine (if adoption not finalized within 18 months); Oklahoma (if adoption petition not filed within 9 months); and Nevada (if prospective adoptive family found to be unsuitable or no petition is filed within 2 years).

RIGHTS OF PUTATIVE FATHERS

There has been a dramatic increase in the number of out-of-wedlock births since the 1960s. Although much focus has been placed on the unwed mothers, the unwed fathers of these children have received little attention, and far fewer rights, until recently.

"Putative" father is the legal term for the alleged or supposed father of a child. There are a growing number of putative fathers who now seek to play a role in their children's upbringing. Thus, their legal rights in custody and visitation matters have become increasingly important.

Constitutional Rights

Historically, putative fathers have had fewer rights with regard to their children than either unwed mothers or married parents. However, over the past several decades, putative fathers have used the Fourteenth Amendment to challenge the termination of their parental rights when the birth mother relinquishes their child for adoption.

Nevertheless, states have almost complete discretion to determine the rights of a putative father at proceedings to terminate parental rights or adoption proceedings. Further, there is a lack of uniformity among states as to the level of protection available to unwed fathers.

The U.S. Supreme Court has affirmed the constitutional protection of a putative father's parental rights when he has established a substantial relationship with his child. The Court has defined a substantial relationship as the existence of a biological link between the child and putative father, and it defined the father's commitment to the responsibilities of parenthood as participating in the child's upbringing (Stanley v. Illinois, 405 U.S. 645 (1972); Quilloin v. Walcott, 434 U.S. 246 (1978); Caban v. Mohammed, 441 U.S. 380 (1979); Lehr v. Robertson, 463 U.S. 248 (1983)).

Although it is easy to prove a biological link to the child through a paternity test, it is far more difficult for a putative father to meet the other criteria set forth by the court because the father does not have the opportunity to develop a substantial relationship with a child who has been placed for adoption at birth.

Putative Father Registries

In almost all jurisdictions, putative fathers are entitled to notice of proceedings to terminate parental rights or adoption proceedings. However, states generally require a putative father to register with the state putative father registry, or acknowledge paternity within a certain time frame, in order to receive notice of such proceedings.

Approximately 23 states have statutes authorizing the establishment of a putative father registry. Those states include: Alabama, Arizona, Arkansas, Delaware, Florida, Georgia, Idaho, Illinois, Indiana, Iowa, Louisiana, Minnesota, Missouri, Montana, Nebraska, New Hampshire, New Mexico, New York, Ohio, Oklahoma, Tennessee, Texas, and Wyoming.

Information Maintained in Registries

Although the information maintained in a putative father registry varies by state, it generally includes the following:

1. The name, address, social security number, and date of birth of the putative father and birth mother;

2. The name and address of any person adjudicated by a court to be the child's father;

3. The child's name and date of birth or expected month and year of birth;

4. The registration date; and

5. Any other information deemed necessary.

Access to Registry Information

Access to information maintained in a putative father registry varies from state to state. In general, those who have a direct interest in the case are entitled to access, including the following:

1. Birth mothers;

2. Courts;

3. Attorneys;

4. Licensed adoption agencies;

5. Prospective adoptive parents;

6. State departments or divisions of social services;

7. State offices of child support enforcement;

8. Any other person upon a court order for good cause shown; and

9. Putative father registries of other states.

Revocation of Paternity Claim

Approximately 22 states have statutory provisions that allow putative fathers to revoke or rescind their notice of intent to claim paternity. These states include: Alabama, Alaska, Arkansas, Connecticut, Delaware, Florida, Georgia, Indiana, Iowa, Maine, Missouri, Montana, Nebraska, New Mexico, New York, Oklahoma, Oregon, Pennsylvania, Tennessee, Texas, Washington, and Wyoming.

Of these states, Delaware, Indiana, Missouri, Montana, Nebraska, New Mexico, New York, Oklahoma, Tennessee, Texas, and Wyoming allow revocation at any time, while revocation is effective only after the child's birth in Arkansas and Iowa. Florida only allows revocation at any time prior to the child's birth.

In Alaska, Connecticut, Georgia, Maine, Oregon, Pennsylvania, and Washington, the right of rescission is limited to 60 days after the paternity claim is submitted, or prior to a court proceeding to establish paternity, whichever occurs first. Most states will accept a written, notarized statement for rescission. Washington, however, requires a court proceeding for revocation of a paternity claim.

A table of state statutes governing the rights of putative fathers is set forth in Appendix 11.

TERMINATION OF PARENTAL RIGHTS

Before a child can be legally adopted, his or her birth parent's rights must be terminated. As discussed above, birth parents who wish to place their children for adoption may voluntarily relinquish their rights. A judge can also terminate parental rights involuntarily, based on state law. All states and the District of Columbia have statutes providing for the termination of parental rights.

Termination of parental rights ends the legal parent-child relationship. Once the relationship has been terminated, the child is legally free to be placed for adoption with the objective of securing a more stable, permanent family environment that can meet the child's long-term parenting needs.

When addressing whether parental rights should be terminated involuntarily, most states require that a court:

1. Determine a parent to be unfit through one or more grounds for termination of the parental relationship; and

2. Determine whether severing the parent-child relationship will be in the child's best interest.

The U.S. Supreme Court set the standard of proof in termination of parental rights proceedings as "by clear and convincing evidence" (Santosky v. Kramer, 455 U.S.§ 745(1982)).

Grounds for Termination

The grounds for termination of parental rights are based on circumstances that demonstrate: (1) a risk of harm to the child if he or she is returned home; or (2) the inability of the parent to provide for the child's basic needs.

Some states set forth specific factors that constitute grounds for termination of parental rights while other states use general language. The most common statutory grounds for involuntary termination of parental rights include:

1. Severe or chronic abuse or neglect;

2. Abuse or neglect of other children in the household;

3. Abandonment;

4. Long-term mental illness or deficiency of the parent(s);

5. Long-term alcohol- or drug-induced incapacity of the parent(s);

6. Failure to support or maintain contact with the child;

7. Involuntary termination of rights of the parent to another child;

8. A felony conviction of the parent(s) for a crime of violence against the child or another family member;

9. A conviction for any felony when the term of incarceration is such a length of time as to have a negative impact on the child, and the only available provision of care for the child is foster care.

The above factors become grounds for terminating parental rights when reasonable efforts by the state to prevent out-of-home placement, or to achieve reunification of the family after placement, has failed to correct the conditions and/or parental behaviors that led to state intervention.

Requirements for Termination under the Adoption and Safe Families Act

The Adoption and Safe Families Act (ASFA) requires state agencies to seek termination of the parent-child relationship when:

1. A child has been in foster care for 15 of the most recent 22 months; or

2. A court has determined that:

(a) the child is an abandoned infant; or

(b) the parent has (i) committed murder or voluntary manslaughter of another child of the parent; (ii) aided, abetted, attempted, conspired, or solicited to commit such a murder or voluntary manslaughter; or (iii) committed a felony assault that has resulted in serious bodily injury to the child or another child of the parent.

In response to ASFA, many states have adopted limits to the maximum amount of time a child can spend in foster care before termination proceedings must be initiated.

Typically, states have adopted the ASFA standard of 15 out of the most recent 22 months in care. Some States, however, specify shorter time limits, particularly for very young children. The laws in most states are consistent with the other termination grounds required under ASFA.

Exceptions to Termination

Even when there are sufficient grounds for terminating a parent's parental rights, a petition to terminate may not always be required under some circumstances. These circumstances may include:

1. The child has been placed under the care of a relative;

2. There is a compelling reason to believe that terminating the parent's rights is not in the best interests of the child; or

3. The parent has not been provided with the services required by the service plan for reunification of the parent with the child.

INFANT SAFE HAVEN LAWS

Under present law, a woman faced with an unwanted pregnancy may obtain an abortion if it is carried out within the legally permissible time period. If the woman does not want an abortion, she can keep the newborn or choose to place the infant for adoption. Historically, it was illegal to simply abandon a baby, and the parent faced criminal charges, including murder, if the infant died. However, despite the prohibition, infants were discarded, left alone in unsafe and life-threatening situations, or otherwise deserted by mothers who were unwilling or unable to handle motherhood.

In response to a reported increase in infant abandonment and infant homicide, state legislatures began to enact legislation that would allow a parent, or an agent of the parent, to avoid prosecution for abandonment or neglect if they surrendered the unwanted infant to a designated "safe haven." The goal of the legislation is to protect newborns and provide mothers in crisis an alternative to abandonment.

Infant safe haven laws—also known as "Baby Moses laws"—have been passed in approximately 46 states to date. The specific provisions vary according to the state. In most states, either parent, or an agent of the parent, may surrender the infant to a safe haven; however, Georgia, Maryland, Minnesota and Tennessee require the mother to relinquish the infant. Most states require the parent to relinquish the infant within a certain time period, generally within a certain number of days following birth.

Safe Haven Providers

The laws also designate the facilities that may serve as safe havens, and include hospitals, emergency medical services, and police and fire stations. These safe havens are authorized to provide medical care and treatment to the abandoned infant, and are generally granted immunity from liability for anything that may happen to the infant while in their care.

The parent relinquishing the child is generally guaranteed anonymity, and any information offered is kept confidential. Nevertheless, many states require the safe haven provider to request family and medical history information from the parent, and provide information concerning their legal rights, e.g. to reclaim the infant. The parent, however, is not compelled to either provide or accept any information.

Custody of the infant is usually transferred to the department that handles child protection soon after the child is relinquished. The department is responsible for petitioning the court for termination of parental rights and placing the child for adoption. A number of states set forth the procedures the relinquishing parent must follow in order to reclaim the child, however, this must generally take place before parental rights have been terminated by court order.

Unintended Negative Consequences

Infant safe haven laws have been criticized by some organizations as ineffective. An extensive study conducted by the Evan Donaldson Adoption Institute, a non-profit organization whose stated mission is to improve adoption policy and practice, has found that safe haven laws do not solve the problem of unsafe infant abandonment, in large part because they do not address the causes of the problem.

Further, the Adoption Institute study has concluded that, in addition to undermining adoptions conducted through established legal procedures, infant safe haven laws have resulted in a number of unintended negative consequences. According to the study, infant safe haven laws:

1. Create the opportunity for upset family members, disgruntled boyfriends, or others who have no legal rights, to abandon babies without the mothers' consent;

2. Induce abandonment by women who otherwise would not have done so because it is perceived as "easier" than receiving parenting counseling or making an adoption plan;

3. Deprive biological fathers of their legal right to care for their sons or daughters, even if they have the desire and personal resources to do so;

4. Ensure that the children who are abandoned can never learn their genealogical or medical histories, even when the consequences for their health are dire;

5. Preclude the possibility of contact and/or the exchange of medical or personal information between birth parents and children in the future; and

6. Send a signal, especially to young people, that they do not necessarily have to assume responsibility for their actions and that deserting one's children is acceptable.

The Adoption Institute study advocates further research into the causes of abandonment, educational, and counseling in order to devise a better policy response to the problem of infant abandonment.

A table of state Infant Safe Haven Laws is set forth in Appendix 12.

CHAPTER 6:
POST-ADOPTION CONSIDERATIONS

POST-ADOPTION CONTACT AGREEMENTS

A post-adoption contact agreement—also referred to as an "open adoption agreement"—is a court-approved contract that permits some degree of continuing contact or communication between the child's adoptive family and the child's birth family after the adoption is finalized. The type of contact agreed to can range anywhere from the mere exchange of information about the child between the adoptive and birth parents to personal visits with the child by birth family members.

Post-adoption contact agreements have become more common recently for several reasons. For example, many adoptions involve older children, such as stepchildren or foster children, who have had some type of ongoing contact with their birth relatives. It is recognized that continuing such a relationship is beneficial for the child. In addition, contact between the adoptive family and the birth family can be a valuable resource if birth family information is needed, e.g., for medical reasons.

Parties to the Agreement

Most statutes permit post-adoption contact or communication for birth parents. Some states also allow other birth relatives who have significant emotional ties to the child to be included in an agreement, including grandparents, aunts, uncles, or siblings. Minnesota permits foster parents to petition for contact privileges. California, Florida, Indiana, Louisiana, and Maryland have provisions for sibling participation in an agreement.

Enforceability

State law does not prohibit post-adoption contact insofar as the adoptive parents have the right to decide who may be in contact with their adopted child. Oftentimes, such ongoing communication is agreed to and arranged on an informal basis; however, enforceability is questionable should the adoptive parents decide to end such contact.

If the parties desire a more formal written agreement to ensure ongoing communication, a written contract, signed by both parties, can specify the type and frequency of the contact, and may be enforceable in court, depending on the state in which the contract was written.

For the agreement to be enforceable, it must be approved by the court that has jurisdiction over the adoption. All parties wishing to be included in the agreement must agree, in writing, to all of the terms of the agreement prior to the adoption finalization. The court may approve the agreement only if all parties, including a child over the age of 12, agree to its provisions. In addition, the terms of the agreement, e.g., the type and frequency of contact, must be in the best interests of the child, and must protect the safety of the child and all parties to the agreement.

Presently, approximately 22 states have statutes that allow written and enforceable post-adoption contact agreements, including Arizona, California, Connecticut, Florida, Indiana, Louisiana, Maryland, Massachusetts, Minnesota, Montana, Nebraska, Nevada, New Hampshire, New Mexico, New York, Oklahoma, Oregon, Rhode Island, Texas, Vermont, Washington, and West Virginia.

Connecticut and Nebraska limit the application of agreements to children who have been adopted while in foster care. Indiana limits enforceable contact agreements to children aged 2 and older. For children under age 2, non-enforceable agreements are permitted as long as the type of contact does not include visitation.

Resolving Disputes and Mediation

Disputes over compliance and requests for modification of the terms of a post-adoption contact agreement must also be brought before the court having jurisdiction over the adoption. Any party to the agreement may petition the court to modify, order compliance with, or void the agreement. The court may do so only if the parties agree or circumstances have changed, and the action is determined to be in the best interests of the child. In no case can disputes over the post-adoption contact agreement be used as grounds for setting aside an adoption or relinquishment of parental rights.

Nine states, including Arizona, California, Connecticut, Louisiana, Minnesota, New Hampshire, Oklahoma, Oregon, and Texas, require the parties to participate in mediation before a petition for enforcement or modification of an agreement is brought before the court. In Florida and Maryland, the court, at its discretion, may refer the parties to mediation. In Massachusetts, any party seeking to enforce an agreement may voluntarily choose mediation.

States Without Enforceable Post-Adoption Agreements

In most states that do not have enforceable post-adoption contact agreements, the statutes are silent about the issue of post-adoption contact or communication. Approximately eight other states address the issue but do not provide for enforceable agreements, as discussed below.

Alaska's statute merely states that contact agreements are not prohibited and, in Vermont, agreements for contact are enforceable only in cases involving stepparent adoptions. North Carolina permits agreements by mutual consent, but specifies that they are not enforceable, and failure to comply is not grounds to invalidate consent to the adoption.

Ohio, South Carolina, and South Dakota specifically state that mutual agreements for contact are nonbinding and nonenforceable. Finally, Missouri and Tennessee leave decisions about contact and visitation with birth relatives to the sole discretion of the adoptive parents.

ACCESS TO ADOPTION RECORDS

In almost all states, adoption records are sealed and withheld from public inspection after the adoption is finalized. However, most states have established procedures by which parties to an adoption may obtain non-identifying and identifying information from an adoption record while still protecting the interests of all parties, as further discussed below. Policies on what information is collected and how that information is maintained and disclosed vary from state to state.

Non-Identifying Information

Non-identifying information is generally limited to descriptive details about an adopted person and the adopted person's birth relatives, and is provided to the adoptive parents at the time of the adoption. Non-identifying information may include the following:

1. Date and place of the adopted person's birth;

2. Age of the birth parents and their general physical description, such as eye color and hair color;

3. Race, ethnicity, religion, and medical history of the birth parents;

4. Educational level of the birth parents;

5. The occupation of the birth parents at the time of the adoption;

6. The reason for placing the child for adoption; and

7. The existence of other children born to each birth parent.

Non-identifying information generally includes medical and health information about the child and the child's birth family at the time of the adoptive placement. The statutes in Alabama, Illinois, Kansas, Maryland, Minnesota, Mississippi, and Wyoming allow the adoptive parents to request the department to contact the birth parents any time post-adoption for additional health information when there is a medical need.

All states have statutory provisions that allow access to non-identifying information by an adoptive parent or a guardian of an adopted person who is still a minor. Nearly all states allow the adopted person to have access to non-identifying information about birth relatives, generally upon written request. However, the adopted person must be an adult, usually at least 18 years of age, before he or she may access this information. Nevertheless, California, Idaho, Nevada, and New Jersey allow access to this information to the adoptive parents only.

Approximately 27 states allow birth parents access to non-identifying information. The states that allow birth parents access to non-identifying information include: Alabama, Arizona, Arkansas, Colorado, Connecticut, Delaware, Louisiana, Maryland, Massachusetts, Michigan, Mississippi, Montana, New Hampshire, New Mexico, New York, North Dakota, Ohio, Oklahoma, Oregon, Pennsylvania, Rhode Island, South Carolina, Tennessee, Utah, Vermont, Washington, and West Virginia.

In addition, many states allow access to non-identifying information to adult birth siblings. States that allow access to adult birth siblings include: Arizona, Colorado, Michigan, Mississippi, Montana, New Mexico, New York, North Carolina, Ohio, Oklahoma, Rhode Island, South Carolina, Utah, and Vermont.

Restrictions on the Release of Non-Identifying Information

There are a few jurisdictions that are more restrictive concerning the release of information from adoption records. For example, New York, Oklahoma, and Rhode Island require the person seeking non-identifying information to register with the state adoption registry. Pennsylvania requires a party to petition the court before any information can be released.

Identifying Information

Identifying information is any data that may lead to the positive identification of an adopted person, birth parents, or other birth relatives, including the current name of the person. Identifying information usually also includes an address or other contact information so that adopted persons and birth relatives can arrange personal contact.

The statutes in nearly all states permit the release of identifying information when the person whose information is sought has consented to the release. However, New Jersey and the District of Columbia require a court order for the release of identifying information.

Many states ask birth parents to specify, at the time they consent to adoption or relinquish their child, whether they are willing to have their identity disclosed to the adopted child when he or she reaches the age of 18 or 21. If consent is not on file, the information may not be released without a court order documenting good cause to release the information. The person seeking a court order must be able to demonstrate, by clear and convincing evidence, that there is a compelling reason for disclosure that outweighs maintaining the confidentiality of a party to the adoption.

Access to information is not always restricted to birth parents and children. Approximately 33 states allow biological siblings of the adopted individual to seek and release identifying information upon mutual consent. These states include: Arizona, Arkansas, California, Connecticut, Florida, Georgia, Idaho, Illinois, Indiana, Iowa, Kentucky, Louisiana, Maine, Maryland, Michigan, Minnesota, Missouri, Montana, Nevada, New Mexico, New York, North Dakota, Ohio, Oklahoma, Oregon, Rhode Island, South Carolina, Tennessee, Texas, Utah, Vermont, Virginia, and Wyoming.

Restrictions on the Release of Identifying Information

Some states have imposed restrictions on the release of identifying information. For example, Arkansas, Mississippi, South Carolina, and Texas require the adopted person to undergo counseling about the possible consequences of contact with his or her birth family before any information is disclosed. In Connecticut, the release of identifying information is prohibited if it is determined that the requested information would be seriously disruptive to any of the parties involved.

Mutual Consent Registries

A mutual consent registry is a system whereby individuals directly involved in adoptions can indicate their willingness or unwillingness to have their identifying information disclosed. A mutual consent registry is one method many states use to arrange the consents that are required for the release of identifying information.

Approximately 29 states have established some form of a mutual consent registry. These states include: Arkansas, Colorado, Delaware, Florida, Georgia, Hawaii, Idaho, Illinois, Indiana, Iowa, Louisiana, Maine, Maryland, Michigan, Missouri, Nevada, New York, Ohio, Oklahoma, Oregon, Pennsylvania, Rhode Island, South Carolina, South Dakota, Tennessee, Texas, Utah, Vermont, and West Virginia.

Procedures for mutual consent registries vary significantly from state to state. Most registries require consent of at least one birth parent and an adopted person over the age of 18 or 21, or of adoptive parents if the adopted person is still a minor, in order to release identifying information.

Most of the states that have registries require the parties seeking to exchange information to file affidavits consenting to release of their personal information. However, eight states will release information from the registry upon request, unless the affected party has filed an affidavit requesting nondisclosure. The states that will release identifying information unless a non-consent affidavit has been filed include: Hawaii; Indiana (for adoptions finalized after 12/31/1993); Maryland (for adoptions finalized after 1/1/2000); Michigan (for adoptions finalized before 5/28/1948 or after 9/12/1980); Minnesota (for adoptions finalized after 8/1/1982); Nebraska (for adoptions finalized after 9/1/1998); Ohio; and Vermont (for adoptions finalized after 7/1/1986).

Other Methods of Obtaining Consent

States that have not established registries may use alternative methods for disclosing identifying information. Search and consent procedures authorize a public or private agency to assist a party in locating birth family members to determine if they consent to the release of information.

Some states have a type of search and consent procedure called a confidential intermediary system. In this system, an individual called a confidential intermediary is certified by the court to have access to sealed adoption records for the purpose of conducting a search for birth family members to obtain their consent for contact.

The states using confidential intermediaries include: Alabama (when consent is not on file); Colorado; Illinois (to obtain updated medical information); Michigan (when consent is not on file); Montana; Oklahoma; and Washington.

Other states use an affidavit system through which birth family members can file either their consent or non-consent to the release of identifying information, and their refusal to be contacted. These states include: Alabama, Alaska, Arizona, California, Connecticut, Kentucky, Massachusetts, Minnesota, Mississippi, Nebraska, New Hampshire, New Mexico, North Carolina, and Wisconsin.

Original Birth Certificate

When an adoption is finalized, a new birth certificate for the child is customarily issued to the adoptive parents. The original birth certificate is then sealed and kept confidential by the state registrar of vital records.

In the past, nearly all states required a court order for adopted persons to gain access to their original birth certificates.

In approximately 29 states and the District of Columbia, a court order is still required to gain access to the original birth certificate. These states include: Arizona, Arkansas, California, Connecticut, Florida, Georgia, Hawaii, Iowa, Kansas, Kentucky, Louisiana, Maine, Massachusetts, Missouri, Nevada, New Hampshire, New Jersey, New Mexico, New York, North Carolina, North Dakota, Oregon, South Carolina, South Dakota, Texas, Utah, Virginia, West Virginia, and Wyoming.

Nevertheless, in many states, the laws are changing to allow easier access to these records. Some of the methods now available include:

1. Records are available through court order when all parties have consented in Idaho and Mississippi;

2. Records are available upon request to the adult adopted person in Alabama (at age 19) and Alaska (at age 18);

3. Records are available upon request to the adopted person unless the birth parent has filed an affidavit denying release of confidential records in Delaware; Montana (for adoptions finalized on or after 10/1/1997); Nebraska (for adopted adults age 25 or older); Maryland (for adoptions finalized on or after 1/1/2000); Nebraska (for adoptions finalized on or after 7/20/2002); Ohio; Oklahoma (for adoptions finalized on or after 11/1/1997 and there are no birth siblings under age 18 who have been adopted); and Washington (for adoptions finalized on or after 10/1/1993).

4. Records are available to persons who have established their eligibility to receive identifying information through a state adoption registry in Illinois (for adoptions finalized after 1/1/2000); Indiana (for adoptions finalized after 12/31/1993); Michigan; Rhode Island; Tennessee; and Vermont.

5. Records are available when consents to the release of identifying information from the birth parents are on file in Colorado; Nebraska (for adoptions finalized on or after 9/1/1998); Pennsylvania; and Wisconsin.

INHERITANCE RIGHTS OF ADOPTED CHILDREN

When a person dies without leaving a valid will, this is known as dying "intestate." Thus, the best way to make sure your property is distributed according to your wishes is to make a will and designate your beneficiaries. The will of a birth parent or adoptive parent will specify whether the parent has left any property to the adopted child. However, when a birth parent or adoptive parent dies intestate, the rights of the adopted child to inherit from either parent must be examined according to the state's intestate inheritance laws.

Birth Parents and the Adopted Child

In general, when a child is legally adopted, this ends the legal relationship between the adopted child and the birth parent. The child is not entitled to inherit from a birth parent who dies intestate, and vice versa, unless an exception exists under state law, as follows:

1. In Alaska, Idaho, Illinois, and Maine, there is a continuation of inheritance rights if it is set forth in the adoption decree.

2. In Kansas, Louisiana, Rhode Island, Texas, and Wyoming, an adoption decree terminates the right of the birth parent to inherit from the adopted person, but the adopted person may still inherit from the birth parent.

3. In Colorado, if there are no other heirs, the adopted child may file a claim against the estate of the birth parent within 90 days of the birth parent's death.

4. In Illinois, the birth parents may acquire from the adopted child's estate any property gained from them through gift, will, or under state intestate laws.

5. In Pennsylvania, an adopted person may inherit from the estate of a birth relative, other than a birth parent, who has maintained a family relationship with the adopted person.

6. In general, if a child is adopted by the spouse of a birth parent, this has no effect on the right of the child to inherit from or through either birth parent.

Adoptive Parents and the Adopted Child

By law, when a child is legally adopted, he or she becomes the natural child of the adoptive parents. Thereafter, the adopted child has the right to inherit from the adoptive parents and the adoptive parents' relatives. In addition, the adoptive parents and the adoptive parents' relatives gain the right to inherit from the adopted child.

A table of state laws governing intestate inheritance rights of adopted children is set forth in Appendix 13.

CHAPTER 7:
INTERNATIONAL ADOPTION

IN GENERAL

There are many citizens in the United States who have hopes of adopting a child. However, there are fewer and fewer children in America who are available for adoption. Therefore, many citizens have looked to countries outside of the United States for children who are in need of adoptive families. Thousands of children are brought to the United States each year by parents who have either adopted them abroad, or who seek to finalize an adoption of a foreign-born child in America. According to the U.S. Department of State, in 2005, 22,728 children received visas to come to the United States for adoption, compared to only about 7,000 children in 1990.

Unlike the domestic adoptions discussed in this Almanac, the adoption of a foreign-born child by an individual or couple is a private legal matter that is carried out under the laws and regulations of a foreign government. However, the process is not as easy as selecting a child and then simply bringing the child back to live with the adoptive parents in the United States. Procedures have been established which are designed to protect the child, the adoptive parent, and the birth parent.

Adoption procedures vary according to the country. In general, most foreign countries require that the adoptive child is legally recognized as an orphan or, if there is a living parent, that the child is legally and irrevocably released for adoption by the parent. Most countries also require that the adoption proceeding be completed in the foreign court. In addition, some countries require a period of residence by one or both adoptive parents. In these countries, prospective adoptive parents may find it necessary to spend an extended period of time in the foreign country awaiting the completion of the foreign adoption documents.

Some countries do allow for a "simple adoption," which means that the adoptive parent can be granted guardianship of the child by the foreign court. This allows the child to leave the foreign country so that the adoption proceedings can be completed in the country of the adoptive parents. A minority of countries allow adoptive parents to adopt through a third party without actually traveling to that country.

Nevertheless, it is important to note that a foreign country's determination that the child is an orphan does not guarantee that the child will be considered an orphan under governing United States law—The Immigration and Nationality Act (INA)—since the foreign country may use different standards to make this determination.

In most cases, the formal adoption of a child in a foreign court is legally acceptable in the United States. However, a state court is not automatically required to recognize a foreign adoption decree and the status of the adopted child may be subject to challenge in a state court unless an adoption decree is entered in a state in the United States. To prevent any challenges to the validity of the foreign adoption, it is recommended that a child adopted abroad be re-adopted in the court of the adoptive parent's state of residence as a precautionary measure. Once the child is re-adopted in the state court, the adoptive parents can request that a state birth certificate be issued, which will be recognized in all other states.

Under certain circumstances, the re-adoption of a foreign-born adopted child is required under U.S. law. This is the case, for example, when the adoptive parent, or one of the adoptive parents if it is a married couple, did not see the child prior to or during the foreign adoption process. In that case, the child must be re-adopted in the United States even if a full final adoption decree has been issued in the foreign country.

It is crucial that all of these issues be considered prior to initiating the adoption process. Therefore, the prospective adoptive parent is advised to consult with an attorney who is fully familiar with both the laws of the foreign country where the child resides, and the requirements under United States law.

CHOOSING THE COUNTRY

It is important to carefully consider the foreign country from which one chooses to adopt a child. Some countries do not permit adoption and will grant legal custody only so long as the applicant for custody resides in that country. This is often the case in countries that apply Islamic law, and children from such countries do not qualify for immigrant status in the United States.

Many prospective adoptive parents are admirably concerned for the health and welfare of children who live in unstable countries where there exists social and political upheaval. However, adopting a child from a country embroiled in chaos may be extremely difficult to complete. For example, it may be difficult to locate documents necessary to fulfill the legal requirements for adoption and immigration to the United States.

In addition, when a parent is missing, it is often difficult to determine whether the child is truly an orphan or whether the child has been temporarily abandoned or involuntarily separated from a parent caught up in a hostile situation. Further, there is a greater chance that the prospective adoptive parent will be taken advantage of by unscrupulous parties who may provide false documentation or otherwise try to process an illegal adoption for financial gain.

These problems can lead to lengthy delays and emotional anguish if the adoption process falls through and/or the adopted child is not permitted to enter the United States. Thus, when considering the adoption of a child from a country in social or political crisis, the prospective adoptive parent is strongly cautioned to contact the U.S. Department of State (DOS) and the U.S. Bureau of Citizenship and Immigration Services (BCIS), an agency organized under the Department of Homeland Security, for further information concerning the particular country before going forward with the adoption process.

ELIGIBILITY TO ADOPT A FOREIGN-BORN CHILD

As previously stated, the adoption of a foreign-born child by an individual or couple is a private legal matter that is carried out under the laws and regulations of a foreign government. However, it is important to note that simply adopting a foreign-born child in a foreign country does not guarantee that the adopted child will gain entry into the United States.

As set forth below, following a foreign adoption, only a U.S. citizen may file a petition with the BCIS for the immediate immigration of the adopted child to the United States. There is no way an orphan can legally immigrate to the United States without being processed through, and approved by the BCIS.

Foreign Adoption by a United States Citizen

Under the INA, an unmarried U.S. citizen who is at least twenty-five years of age, or a married U.S. citizen and his or her spouse, of any age, may file a petition for the immigration of an adopted child to the

United States. The spouse of a married citizen does not have to be a citizen, but must be legally in this country and also agree to the adoption.

The Two-Year Co-Residency Provision

The INA provides immigrant classification for "a child adopted while under the age of sixteen years if the child has been in the legal custody of, and has resided with, the adoptive parent for at least two years." This provision is generally referred to as the "two-year provision," and usually pertains to U.S. citizens who are temporarily residing abroad and wish to adopt a child in accordance with the laws of the foreign country where they reside. In such cases, the two-year co-residency requirement will be satisfied while the adoptive parent and child reside abroad.

The Orphan Petition

The Equal Employment Opportunity Commission ("EEOC") is a federal agency responsible for issuing regulations to enforce the provisions of Title I of the ADA, under the same procedures now applicable to race, color, sex, national origin, and religious discrimination under Title VII of the Civil Rights Act of 1964, as amended, and the Civil Rights Act of 1991.

Most adoptive parents, however, are not able to spend two years living abroad with the child. Thus, they must acquire immigrant classification for the child under Section 101(b)(1)(F) of the INA, which grants immigrant classification to orphans who have been adopted, or will be adopted by United States citizens. The process is initiated by filing a petition, generally referred to as an "orphan petition," with the BCIS.

Under this provision, both the child and the adoptive parents must satisfy a number of requirements established by the INA and the related regulations, but the two-year residency requirement is eliminated. If the orphan petition is approved, the child is considered to be an immediate relative of a United States citizen, and the child can obtain an immigrant visa immediately without being placed on a visa waiting list. Nevertheless, the child must still qualify for an immigrant visa just like any other foreign-born person.

When the adopted child enters the United States with the immigrant visa, the child is considered to be a lawful permanent resident of the United States, not a U.S. citizen. However, due to recent changes in immigration law, in some situations, a child will automatically become a United States citizen immediately upon admission into the United States as a lawful permanent resident.

Orphan Status

Under the INA, a foreign-born child is defined as an orphan if the child does not have any parents because of the death or disappearance of, abandonment or desertion by, or separation or loss from, both parents. A foreign-born child is also an orphan if his or her sole or surviving parent is not able to take proper care of the child and has, in writing, irrevocably released the child for emigration and adoption.

In order for the child to gain entry to the United States, the orphan petition must be filed before the child's 16th birthday. An exception exists allowing the petition to be filed before the child's 18th birthday if the child is a natural sibling of another orphan or adopted child, and is adopted with or following that child by the same adoptive parents.

Foreign Adoption by a Non-U.S. Citizen

A person who is not a United States citizen, such as a legal permanent resident or long-term nonimmigrant visa holder, may not file a petition for the entry of a foreign-born adopted child to the United States, and will not be able to bring a foreign-born adopted child to the United States. Thus, a non-citizen is strongly advised not to adopt a foreign-born child unless and until they are able to obtain United States citizenship themselves.

Under the INA, a legal permanent resident or long-term nonimmigrant visa holder is permitted to bring their spouse and children with them upon entry to the United States, or provide for their immigration at a later date. The definition of "child" under this provision includes: (1) natural born children; (2) step-children; and (3) adopted children.

However, because the INA defines an "adopted child" as one who has been adopted before the age of sixteen, and who has resided with, and been in the legal custody of, the parent for two years, this two-year co-residency provision acts as a bar to the non-citizen in adopting a foreign-born child.

Thus, whereas a child born abroad to a non-citizen after the non-citizen enters the United States is eligible to receive a dependent visa, a child who is adopted in a foreign country must first meet the two-year co-residency requirement before being eligible to emigrate to the United States. Insofar as the INA does not permit a non-citizen to bring the foreign-born adopted child into the United States to fulfill the two-year co-residency requirement, it is impossible for the child to obtain a dependent visa under the Act.

Long-Term Nonimmigrant Visa Holders

In the case of a nonimmigrant visa holder, in order to have the foreign-born adopted child join them in the United States, the visa holder must leave the United States and live abroad with the adopted child for two years to fulfill the co-residency requirement. The visa holder can then receive a dependent visa for the adopted child for future visits to the United States.

Long-term nonimmigrant visa classes include: E1/E2 Treaty Traders or Investors, F-1 Students, I Journalists, J-1 Exchange Visitors, H, O, or P Visa Temporary Workers, L-1 Intra-company Transfers, and R-1 Religious Workers. Different rules cover diplomats and officials in the United States on A or G visas, and the U.S. Department of State, or embassy or international organization employing the individual should be contacted for further information.

Legal Permanent Residents

In the case of a legal permanent resident, the provisions of the INA produce a more difficult scenario because a legal permanent resident is not permitted to reside outside of the United States. This provision makes it impossible for the legal permanent resident to fulfill the two-year co-residency requirement in order to petition for the adopted child's entry into the United States.

Nevertheless, once a legal permanent resident naturalizes as a United States citizen, he or she may petition for the immediate immigration of a foreign-born adopted, or prospective adopted, child to the United States.

ROLE OF THE U.S. GOVERNMENT IN INTERNATIONAL ADOPTION

Although a number of agencies of the United States government provide information to prospective adoptive parents on the various aspects of the foreign adoption process, United States authorities do not get involved on the parent's behalf with the courts in the country where the adoption is supposed to take place.

The U.S. Department of State

As set forth below, the U.S. Department of State (DOS) provides detailed information on the adoption process in various foreign countries. Because international adoption is a private matter between the prospective adoptive parents and a sovereign foreign country, the DOS cannot intervene in the foreign courts on behalf of the parents, however, the DOS does provide the following information and services:

1. The DOS can provide information about international adoption in over 60 foreign countries;

2. The DOS can provide information about U.S. visa requirements for international adoption;

3. The DOS can make inquiries of the U.S. consular section abroad regarding the status of a specific adoption case, and clarify documentation or other requirements; and

4. The DOS can ensure that U.S. citizens are not discriminated against by foreign authorities or courts.

The DOS cannot undertake any of the following actions:

1. Title I: Employment–Title I of the ADA prohibits discrimination against disabled persons in all aspects of employment, and requires businesses to provide reasonable accommodations to these individuals. Title I is discussed in more detail in Chapter 2, Types of Adoption, of this Almanac.

1. The DOS cannot locate a child available for adoption;

2. The DOS cannot become directly involved in the adoption process in another country;

3. The DOS cannot act as an attorney or represent adoptive parents in court; and

4. The DOS cannot order that an adoption take place or that a visa be issued.

The Office of Children's Issues, a division of the Department of State's Bureau of Consular Affairs, formulates, develops and coordinates policies and programs and provides direction to foreign service posts on international adoption.

Adoption information is made available on a 24 hour basis through the DOS website (http://travel.state.gov/); via recorded telephone information at (202) 736-7000; and through an automated facsimile system at (202) 312-9743.

Written requests for information on international adoption may be sent to the DOS at the following address:

Office of Children's Issues
U.S. Department of State

CA/OCS/CI
1800 G Street, NW, Suite 2100
Washington, D.C. 20006

International adoption procedures are discussed more fully in this author's legal Almanac entitled International Adoption.

APPENDIX 1:
TABLE OF STATE ADOPTION STATUTES

STATE	STATUTE
Alabama	Alabama Code, Title 26, Chapter 10
Alaska	Alaska Statutes, Chapter 23, §§ 5 through 240
Arizona	Arizona Revised Statutes, Title 8, §§ 8-101 through 8-173
Arkansas	Arkansas Ann. Code, Title 9, Subtitle 2, Chapter 9
California	California Family Code, §§ 7660-9300
Colorado	Colorado Revised Statutes, Title 19, Article 5, Part 2
Connecticut	Connecticut Ann. Statutes, HB 5349, 5843, 5966, 6607, 7035, 70076; SB 1274; Chapter 803, §§ 45a-706-45a-770
Delaware	Delaware Ann. Code, Title 13, Chapter 9
District of Columbia	D.C. Code Ann., Division 2, Title 16, Chapter 3
Florida	Florida Ann. Statutes, Title VI, Chapter 63
Georgia	Georgia Ann. Code, §§ 19-1-1 through 19-15-7
Hawaii	Hawaii Revised Statutes, Chapter 578
Idaho	Idaho Ann. Code, §§ 16-1501 through 16-1515
Illinois	Illinois Comp. Statutes, Chapter 750, Act 50
Indiana	Indiana Ann. Code, Title 31, Article 19
Iowa	Iowa Ann. Statutes, Chapter 600

STATE	STATUTE
Kansas	Kansas Ann. Statutes, Chapter 59, Article 21
Kentucky	Kentucky Revised Statutes, Title XVII, Chapter 199
Louisiana	Louisiana Children's Code, Title XII
Maine	Maine Revised Statutes, Title 19, Chapter 21
Maryland	Maryland Family Law, 5-301 through 5-4B-12
Massachusetts	Massachusetts Ann. Laws, Chapter 210, §§ 1 through 14
Michigan	Michigan Comp. Laws, Chapter 722, §§ 722.951 through 722.960
Minnesota	Minnesota Ann. Statutes, Chapter 259
Mississippi	Mississippi Ann. Code, Title 93, Chapter 17
Missouri	Missouri Ann. Statutes, Chapter 453
Montana	Montana Ann. Code, Title 42
Nebraska	Nebraska Revised Statutes, Chapter 43
Nevada	Nevada Revised Statutes, Chapter 127
New Hampshire	New Hampshire Revised Statutes, Title 10, Chapter 126D
New Jersey	New Jersey Ann. Statutes, Title 9
New Mexico	New Mexico Ann. Statutes, Chapter 40, Articles 7A, 7B, 14
New York	New York Domestic Relations Law, Chapter 14, Article 7
North Carolina	North Carolina General Statutes, Chapter 48
North Dakota	North Dakota Cent. Code, Chapter 14-15
Ohio	Ohio Revised Code, Title 31, Chapter 3107
Oklahoma	Oklahoma Ann. Statutes, Chapter 10, §§ 7001 through 7501
Oregon	Oregon Revised Statutes, Title 11, Chapter 109
Pennsylvania	Pennsylvania Cons. Statutes, Title 23, Part 2
Rhode Island	Rhode Island General Laws, Chapter 15-7
South Carolina	South Carolina Ann. Laws, Title 20, Chapter 7, Article 11, Subarticle 7

STATE	STATUTE
South Dakota	South Dakota Ann. Code, Title 25, Chapter 6
Tennessee	Tennessee Ann. Code, Title 36, Chapter 1
Texas	Texas Family Code, Title 5, Chapter 162
Utah	Utah Ann. Code, Title 78, Chapter 30
Vermont	Vermont Statutes, Title, 15, Chapter 9
Virginia	Virginia Ann. Code, Title 63.2, Chapters 12 to 14
Washington	Washington Rev. Code, Title 26, Chapter 33
West Virginia	West Virginia Ann. Code, Chapter 48,, Article 4
Wisconsin	Wisconsin Ann. Statutes, Chapter 48.43 through 48.835
Wyoming	Wyoming Ann. Statutes, Title 1, Chapter 22

Source: Legal Information Institute.

APPENDIX 2:
DIRECTORY OF STATE ADOPTION INFORMATION WEBSITES

STATE AGENCY	ADOPTION INFORMATION WEBSITE
Alabama Department of Human Resources	www.dhr.state.al.us/page.asp?pageid =306
Alaska Department of Health and Social Services	www.hss.state.ak.us/ocs/Adoptions/ default.htm
Arizona Department of Economic Security	www.de.state.az.us/dcyf/adoption/ default.asp
Arkansas Department of Human Services	www.sstate.ar.us/dhs/adoption/adoption. html
California Department of Social Services	www.childsworld.ca.gov/CFSDAdopti_ 309.htm
Colorado Department of Human Services	www.changealifeforever.org/adoption.asp
Connecticut Department of Children and Families	www.ct.gov/dcf/cwp/view/ asp?a= 2561& 0=330740
Delaware Department of Services for Children	www.state.de.us/kids/adoption.htm
District of Columbia Child and Family Services Agency	http://Cfsa.dc.gov/cfsa/cwp/view.a.3.q. 520649.asp
Florida Department of Children and Families	www.dcf.state.fl.us/adoption
Georgia Department of Human Services	http://dfcs.dhr.georgia.gov/portal/site/ DHR-DFCS

STATE AGENCY	ADOPTION INFORMATION WEBSITE
Hawaii Department of Human Services	www.hawaii.gov/dhs/protection/social_services
Idaho Department of Health and Welfare	www.healthandwelfare.idaho.gov/portal
Illinois Department of Children and Family Services	www.state.il.us/dcfs/adoption/index.shtml
Indiana Department of Child Services	www.in.gov/dcs/programs/adoption.html
Iowa Department of Human Services	www.dhs.state.ia.us/dhs2005/dhs_homepage
Kansas Department of Social Services	www.srskansas.org/services/adoption.htm
Kentucky Department of Community Based Services	http://chfs.ky.gov/dcbs/dpp/adoptionservices.htm
Louisiana Department of Social Services	www.dss.state.la.us/departments/ocs/Adoption_Services.html
Maine Department of Health and Human Services	www.afamilyforme.org/adopt.html
Maryland Department of Human Resources	www.dhr.state.md.us/ssa/adopt.htm
Massachusetts	www.mass.gov/
Michigan Department of Human Services	www.michigan.gov/dhs
Minnesota Department of Human Services	www.dhs.state.mn.us/main/
Mississippi Department of Human Services	www.state.ms.us
Missouri Department of Social Services	www.dss.mo.gov/cd/adopt.htm
Montana Department of Public Health	www.dphhs.mt.gov/cfsd/adoption/adoptioninmontana.shtml
Nebraska Department of Health and Human Services	www.state.nd.us/humanservices/services/childfamiliy/adoption
Nevada Department of Human Resources	www.dcfs.state.ny.us/DCFS_Adoption.htm
New Hampshire Department of Health	www.dhhs.state.nh.us/DHHS/FCADOPTION/default.htm

STATE AGENCY	ADOPTION INFORMATION WEBSITE
New Jersey Department of Human Services	www.state.nj.us/humanservices/adoption/ adopt.html
New Mexico Department of Children, Youth and Families	www.cyfd.org/index.htm
New York State Office of Children and Family Services	www.ocfs.state.ny.us/adopt
North Carolina Department of Health and Human Services	www.dhhs.state.nc.us/dss/adopt
North Dakota Department of Human Services	www.state.nd.us/humanservices/ services/ childfamily/adoption
Ohio Department of Job and Family Services	http://jfs.ohio.gov/oapl/index.htm
Oklahoma Department of Human Services	www.okdhs.org/adopt
Oregon Department of Human Services	www.oregon.gov/DHS/children/adoption/
Pennsylvania Department of Public Welfare	www.dpw.state.pa.us/Child/Adoption FosterCare/
Rhode Island Department of Children, Youth and Families	www.dcyf.ri.gov/adoption.htm
South Carolina Department of Social Services	www.state.sc.us/dss/adoption/index.html
South Dakota Department of Social Services	http://dss.sd.gov/adoption/
Tennessee Department of Children's Services	http://state.tn.us/youth/adoption.htm
Texas Department of Family and Protective Services	www.tdprs.state.tx.us/Adoption_and_ Foster_Care/

STATE	ADOPTION INFORMATION WEBSITE
Utah Department of Human Services	www.hsdcfs.utah.gov/adoption.htm
Vermont Department for Child and Families	www.projectfamilyvt.org/adoption.html
Virginia Department of Social Services	www.dss.virginnia.gov/family/ap/index.html
Washington Department of Social and Health Services	www1.dshs.wa.gov/ca/adopt/intro.asp
West Virginia Department of Health and Human Resources	www.wvdhr.org/oss/adoption/
Wisconsin Department of Health and Family Services	www.dhfs.state.wi.us/children/adoption/index.htm
Wyoming Department of Family Services	http://dfsweb.state.wy.us/adoption.html

Source: Child Welfare Information Gateway

APPENDIX 3:
UNIFORM ADOPTION ACT (1994)

SECTION 1-101. DEFINITIONS. In this [Act]:

(1) "Adoptee" means an individual who is adopted or is to be adopted.

(2) Adult" means an individual who has attained 18 years of age.

(3) "Agency" means a public or private entity, including the department, that is authorized by the law of this State to place individuals for adoption.

(4) "Child" means a minor or adult son or daughter, by birth or adoption.

(5) "Court," with reference to a court of this State, means the [appropriate court].

(6) "Department" means the [department of social services, or health services, or children's services].

(7) "Guardian" means an individual, other than a parent, appointed by an appropriate court as general guardian or guardian of the person of a minor.

(8) "Legal custody" means the right and duty to exercise continuing general supervision of a minor as authorized by law. The term includes the right and duty to protect, educate, nurture, and discipline the minor and to provide the minor with food, clothing, shelter, medical care, and a supportive environment.

(9) "Minor" means an individual who has not attained 18 years of age.

(10) "Parent" means an individual who is legally recognized as a mother or father or whose consent to the adoption of a minor is

required under Section 2-401(a)(1). The term does not include an individual whose parental relationship to a child has been terminated judicially or by operation of law.

(11) "Person" means an individual, corporation, limited liability company, business trust, estate, trust, partnership, association, agency, joint venture, government, governmental subdivision or instrumentality, public corporation, or any other legal or commercial entity.

(12) "Physical custody" means the physical care and supervision of a minor.

(13) "Place for adoption" means to select a prospective adoptive parent for a minor and transfer physical custody of the minor to the prospective adoptive parent.

(14) "Relative" means a grandparent, great grandparent, sibling, first cousin, aunt, uncle, great-aunt, great-uncle, niece, or nephew of an individual, whether related to the individual by the whole or the half blood, affinity, or adoption. The term does not include an individual's stepparent.

(15) "Relinquishment" means the voluntary surrender to an agency by a minor's parent or guardian, for purposes of the minor's adoption, of the rights of the parent or guardian with respect to the minor, including legal and physical custody of the minor.

(16) "State" means a State of the United States, the District of Columbia, the Commonwealth of Puerto Rico, or any territory or insular possession subject to the jurisdiction of the United States.

(17) "Stepparent" means an individual who is the spouse or surviving spouse of a parent of a child but who is not a parent of the child.

SECTION 1-102. WHO MAY ADOPT OR BE ADOPTED.

Subject to this [Act], any individual may adopt or be adopted by another individual for the purpose of creating the relationship of parent and child between them.

SECTION 1-103. NAME OF ADOPTEE AFTER ADOPTION.

The name of an adoptee designated in a decree of adoption takes effect as specified in the decree.

SECTION 1-104. LEGAL RELATIONSHIP BETWEEN ADOPTEE AND ADOPTIVE PARENT AFTER ADOPTION.

After a decree of adoption becomes final, each adoptive parent and the adoptee have the legal relationship of parent and child and have all the rights and duties of that relationship.

SECTION 1-105. LEGAL RELATIONSHIP BETWEEN ADOPTEE AND FORMER PARENT AFTER ADOPTION.

Except as otherwise provided in Section 4-103, when a decree of adoption becomes final:

(1) the legal relationship of parent and child between each of the adoptee's former parents and the adoptee terminates, except for a former parent's duty to pay arrearages for child support; and

(2) any previous court order for visitation or communication with an adoptee terminates.

SECTION 1-106. OTHER RIGHTS OF ADOPTEE.

A decree of adoption does not affect any right or benefit vested in the adoptee before the decree becomes final.

SECTION 1-107. PROCEEDINGS SUBJECT TO INDIAN CHILD WELFARE ACT.

A proceeding under this [Act] which pertains to an Indian child, as defined in the Indian Child Welfare Act, 25 U.S.C. Sections 1901 et seq., is subject to that Act.

SECTION 1-108. RECOGNITION OF ADOPTION IN ANOTHER JURISDICTION.

A decree or order of adoption issued by a court of any other State which is entitled to full faith and credit in this State, or a decree or order of adoption entered by a court or administrative entity in another country acting pursuant to that country's law or to any convention or treaty on intercountry adoption which the United States has ratified, has the same effect as a decree or order of adoption issued by a court of this State. The rights and obligations of the parties as to matters within the jurisdiction of this State must be determined as though the decree or order were issued by a court of this State.

ARTICLE 2. ADOPTION OF MINORS

PART 1. PLACEMENT OF MINOR FOR ADOPTION

SECTION 2-101. WHO MAY PLACE MINOR FOR ADOPTION.

(a) The only persons who may place a minor for adoption are:

(1) a parent having legal and physical custody of the minor, as provided in subsections (b) and (c);

(2) a guardian expressly authorized by the court to place the minor for adoption;

(3) an agency to which the minor has been relinquished for purposes of adoption; or

(4) an agency expressly authorized to place the minor for adoption by a court order terminating the relationship between the minor and the minor's parent or guardian.

(b) Except as otherwise provided in subsection (c), a parent having legal and physical custody of a minor may place the minor for adoption, even if the other parent has not executed a consent or a relinquishment or the other parent's relationship to the minor has not been terminated.

(c) A parent having legal and physical custody of a minor may not place the minor for adoption if the other parent has legal custody or a right of visitation with the minor and that parent's whereabouts are known, unless that parent agrees in writing to the placement or, before the placement, the parent who intends to place the minor sends notice of the intended placement by certified mail to the other parent's last known address.

(d) An agency authorized under this [Act] to place a minor for adoption may place the minor for adoption, even if only one parent has executed a relinquishment or has had his or her parental relationship to the minor terminated.

SECTION 2-102. DIRECT PLACEMENT FOR ADOPTION BY PARENT OR GUARDIAN.

(a) A parent or guardian authorized to place a minor directly for adoption may place the minor only with a prospective adoptive parent for whom a favorable preplacement evaluation has been prepared pursuant to Sections 2-201 through 2-206 or for whom a preplacement evaluation is not required under Section 2-201 (b) or (c).

(b) A parent or guardian shall personally select a prospective adoptive parent for the direct placement of a minor. Subject to [Article] 7, the parent or guardian may be assisted by another person, including a lawyer, health-care provider, or agency, in locating or transferring legal and physical custody of the minor to a prospective adoptive parent.

(c) A prospective adoptive parent shall furnish a copy of the preplacement evaluation to the parent or guardian and may provide additional information requested by the parent or guardian. The evaluation and any additional information must be edited to exclude identifying information, but information identifying a prospective adoptive parent need not be edited if the individual agrees to its disclosure. Subject to [Article] 7, a prospective adoptive parent may be assisted by another person in locating a minor who is available for adoption.

(d) If a consent to a minor's adoption is not executed at the time the minor is placed for adoption, the parent or guardian who places the minor shall furnish to the prospective adoptive parent a signed writing stating that the transfer of physical custody is for purposes of adoption and that the parent or guardian has been informed of the provisions of this [Act] relevant to placement for adoption, consent, relinquishment, and termination of parental rights. The writing must authorize the prospective adoptive parent to provide support and medical and other care for the minor pending execution of the consent within a time specified in the writing. The prospective adoptive parent shall acknowledge in a signed writing responsibility for the minor's support and medical and other care and for returning the minor to the custody of the parent or guardian if the consent is not executed within the time specified.

(e) A person who provides services with respect to direct placements for adoption shall furnish to an individual who inquires about the person's services a written statement of the person's services and a schedule of fees.

SECTION 2-103. PLACEMENT FOR ADOPTION BY AGENCY.

(a) An agency authorized to place a minor for adoption shall furnish to an individual who inquires about its services a written statement of its services, including the agency's procedure for selecting a prospective adoptive parent for a minor and a schedule of its fees.

(b) An agency that places a minor for adoption shall authorize in writing the prospective adoptive parent to provide support and medical and other care for the minor pending entry of a decree of adoption. The prospective adoptive parent shall acknowledge in writing responsibility for the minor's support and medical and other care.

(c) Upon request by a parent who has relinquished a minor child pursuant to [Part] 4, the agency shall promptly inform the parent as to whether the minor has been placed for adoption, whether a petition for adoption has been granted, denied, or withdrawn, and, if the petition was not granted, whether another placement has been made.

SECTION 2-104. PREFERENCES FOR PLACEMENT WHEN AGENCY PLACES MINOR.

(a) An agency may place a minor for adoption only with an individual for whom a favorable preplacement evaluation has been prepared pursuant to Sections 2-201 through 2-206. Placement must be made:

(1) if the agency has agreed to place the minor with a prospective adoptive parent selected by the parent or guardian, with the individual selected by the parent or guardian;

(2) if the agency has not so agreed, with an individual selected by the agency in accordance with the best interest of the minor.

(b) In determining the best interest of the minor under subsection (a)(2), the agency shall consider the following individuals in order of preference:

(1) an individual who has previously adopted a sibling of the minor and who makes a written request to adopt the minor;

(2) an individual with characteristics requested by a parent or guardian, if the agency agrees to comply with the request and locates the individual within a time agreed to by the parent or guardian and the agency;

(3) an individual who has had physical custody of the minor for six months or more within the preceding 24 months or for half of the minor's life, whichever is less, and makes a written request to adopt the minor;

(4) a relative with whom the minor has established a positive emotional relationship and who makes a written request to adopt the minor; and

(5) any other individual selected by the agency.

(c) Unless necessary to comply with a request under subsection (b)(2), an agency may not delay or deny a minor's placement for adoption solely on the basis of the minor's race, national origin, or ethnic background. A guardian ad litem of a minor or an individual with a favorable preplacement evaluation who makes a written request to an agency to adopt the minor may maintain an action or proceeding for equitable relief against an agency that violates this subsection.

(d) If practicable and in the best interest of minors who are siblings, an agency shall place siblings with the same prospective adoptive parent selected in accordance with subsections (a) through (c).

(e) If an agency places a minor pursuant to subsection (a)(2), an individual described in subsection (b)(3) may commence an action or proceeding within 30 days after the placement to challenge the agency's placement. If the individual proves by a preponderance of the evidence that the minor has substantial emotional ties to the individual and that an adoptive placement of the minor with the individual would be in the best interest of the minor, the court shall place the minor with the individual.

SECTION 2-105. RECRUITMENT OF ADOPTIVE PARENTS BY AGENCY.

An agency receiving public funds pursuant to Title IV-E of the federal Adoption Assistance and Child Welfare Act, 42 U.S.C. Sections 670 et seq., or pursuant to [the State's adoption subsidy program], shall make a diligent search for and actively recruit prospective adoptive parents for minors in the agency's custody who are entitled to funding from those sources and who are difficult to place for adoption because of a special need as described in [the applicable law on minors with special needs]. The department shall prescribe the procedure for recruiting prospective adoptive parents pursuant to this section.

SECTION 2-106. DISCLOSURE OF INFORMATION ON BACKGROUND.

(a) As early as practicable before a prospective adoptive parent accepts physical custody of a minor, a person placing the minor for adoption shall furnish to the prospective adoptive parent a written report containing all of the following information reasonably available from any person who has had legal or physical custody of the minor or who has provided medical, psychological, educational, or similar services to the minor:

(1) a current medical and psychological history of the minor, including an account of the minor's prenatal care, medical condition at birth, any drug or medication taken by the minor's mother during pregnancy, any subsequent medical, psychological, or psychiatric examination and diagnosis, any physical, sexual, or

emotional abuse suffered by the minor, and a record of any immunizations and health care received while in foster or other care;

(2) relevant information concerning the medical and psychological history of the minor's genetic parents and relatives, including any known disease or hereditary predisposition to disease, any addiction to drugs or alcohol, the health of the minor's mother during her pregnancy, and the health of each parent at the minor's birth; and

(3) relevant information concerning the social history of the minor and the minor's parents and relatives, including:

(i) the minor's enrollment and performance in school, results of educational testing, and any special educational needs;

(ii) the minor's racial, ethnic, and religious background, tribal affiliation, and a general description of the minor's parents;

(iii) an account of the minor's past and existing relationship with any individual with whom the minor has regularly lived or visited; and

(iv) the level of educational and vocational achievement of the minor's parents and relatives and any noteworthy accomplishments;

(4) information concerning a criminal conviction of a parent for a felony, a judicial order terminating the parental rights of a parent, and a proceeding in which the parent was alleged to have abused, neglected, abandoned, or otherwise mistreated the minor, a sibling of the minor, or the other parent;

(5) information concerning a criminal conviction or delinquency adjudication of the minor; and

(6) information necessary to determine the minor's eligibility for state or federal benefits, including subsidies for adoption and other financial, medical, or similar assistance.

(b) Before a hearing on a petition for adoption, the person who placed a minor for adoption shall furnish to the prospective adoptive parent a supplemental written report containing information required by subsection (a) which was unavailable before the minor was placed for adoption but becomes reasonably available to the person after the placement.

(c) The court may request that a respondent in a proceeding under [Article] 3, [Part] 5, supply the information required by this section.

(d) A report furnished under this section must indicate who prepared the report and, unless confidentiality has been waived, be edited to exclude the identity of any individual who furnished information or about whom information is reported.

(e) Information furnished under this section may not be used as evidence in any civil or criminal proceeding against an individual who is the subject of the information.

(f) The department shall prescribe forms designed to obtain the specific information sought under this section and shall furnish the forms to a person who is authorized to place a minor for adoption or who provides services with respect to placements for adoption.

SECTION 2-107. INTERSTATE PLACEMENT.

An adoption in this State of a minor brought into this State from another State by a prospective adoptive parent, or by a person who places the minor for adoption in this State, is governed by the laws of this State, including this [Act] and the Interstate Compact on the Placement of Children.

SECTION 2-108. INTERCOUNTRY PLACEMENT.

An adoption in this State of a minor brought into this State from another country by a prospective adoptive parent, or by a person who places the minor for adoption in this State, is governed by this [Act], subject to any convention or treaty on intercountry adoption which the United States has ratified and any relevant federal law.

PART 2. PREPLACEMENT EVALUATION

SECTION 2-201. PREPLACEMENT EVALUATION REQUIRED.

(a) Except as otherwise provided in subsections (b) and (c), only an individual for whom a current, favorable written preplacement evaluation has been prepared may accept custody of a minor for purposes of adoption. An evaluation is current if it is prepared or updated within the 18 months next preceding the placement of the minor with the individual for adoption. An evaluation is favorable if it contains a finding that the individual is suited to be an adoptive parent, either in general or for a particular minor.

(b) A court may excuse the absence of a preplacement evaluation for good cause shown, but the prospective adoptive parent so excused must be evaluated during the pendency of the proceeding for adoption.

(c) A preplacement evaluation is not required if a parent or guardian places a minor directly with a relative of the minor for purposes of adoption, but an evaluation of the relative is required during the pendency of a proceeding for adoption.

SECTION 2-202. PREPLACEMENT EVALUATOR.

(a) Only an individual qualified by [a state-approved licensing, certifying, or other procedure] to make a preplacement evaluation may do so.

(b) An agency from which an individual is seeking to adopt a minor may require the individual to be evaluated by its own qualified employee or independent contractor, even if the individual has received a favorable preplacement evaluation from another qualified evaluator.

SECTION 2-203. TIMING AND CONTENT OF PREPLACEMENT EVALUATION.

(a) An individual requesting a preplacement evaluation need not have located a prospective minor adoptee when the request is made, and the individual may request more than one evaluation.

(b) A preplacement evaluation must be completed within 45 days after it is requested. An evaluator shall expedite an evaluation for an individual who has located a prospective adoptee.

(c) A preplacement evaluation must be based upon a personal interview and visit at the residence of the individual being evaluated, personal interviews with others who know the individual and may have information relevant to the evaluation, and the information required by subsection (d).

(d) A preplacement evaluation must contain the following information about the individual being evaluated:

(1) age and date of birth, nationality, racial or ethnic background, and any religious affiliation;

(2) marital status and family history, including the age and location of any child of the individual and the identity of and relationship to anyone else living in the individual's household;

(3) physical and mental health, and any history of abuse of alcohol or drugs;

(4) educational and employment history and any special skills;

(5) property and income, including outstanding financial obligations as indicated in a current credit report or financial statement furnished by the individual;

(6) any previous request for an evaluation or involvement in an adoptive placement and the outcome of the evaluation or placement;

(7) whether the individual has been charged with having committed domestic violence or a violation of [the State's child protection statute], and the disposition of the charges, or whether the individual is subject to a court order restricting the individual's right to custody or visitation with a child;

(8) whether the individual has been convicted of a crime other than a minor traffic violation;

(9) whether the individual has located a parent interested in placing a minor with the individual for adoption and, if so, a brief description of the parent and the minor; and

(10) any other fact or circumstance that may be relevant in determining whether the individual is suited to be an adoptive parent, including the quality of the environment in the individual's home and the functioning of other children in the individual's household.

(e) An individual being evaluated must submit to fingerprinting and sign a release permitting the evaluator to obtain from an appropriate law enforcement agency any record indicating that the individual has been convicted of a crime other than a minor traffic violation.

(f) An individual being evaluated shall, at the request of the evaluator, sign any release necessary for the evaluator to obtain information required by subsection (d).

SECTION 2-204. DETERMINING SUITABILITY TO BE ADOPTIVE PARENT.

(a) An evaluator shall assess the information required by Section 2-203 to determine whether it raises a specific concern that placement of any minor, or a particular minor, in the home of the individual would pose a significant risk of harm to the physical or psychological well-being of the minor.

(b) If an evaluator determines that the information assessed does not raise a specific concern, the evaluator shall find that the individual is suited to be an adoptive parent. The evaluator may comment about any factor that in the evaluator's opinion makes the individual suited in general or for a particular minor.

(c) If an evaluator determines that the information assessed raises a specific concern, the evaluator, on the basis of the original or any further investigation, shall find that the individual is or is not suited to be an adoptive parent. The evaluator shall support the finding with a written explanation.

SECTION 2-205. FILING AND COPIES OF PREPLACEMENT EVALUATION.

(a) If a preplacement evaluation contains a finding that an individual is suited to be an adoptive parent, the evaluator shall give the individual a signed copy of the evaluation. At the individual's request, the evaluator shall furnish a copy of the evaluation to a person authorized under this [Act] to place a minor for adoption and, unless the individual requests otherwise, edit the copy to exclude identifying information.

(b) If a preplacement evaluation contains a finding that an individual is not suited to be an adoptive parent of any minor, or a particular minor, the evaluator shall immediately give a signed copy of the evaluation to the individual and to the department. The department shall retain for 10 years the copy and a copy of any court order concerning the evaluation issued pursuant to Section 2-206 or 2-207.

(c) An evaluator shall retain for two years the original of a completed or incomplete preplacement evaluation and a list of every source for each item of information in the evaluation.

(d) An evaluator who conducted an evaluation in good faith is not subject to civil liability for anything contained in the evaluation.

SECTION 2-206. REVIEW OF EVALUATION.

(a) Within 90 days after an individual receives a preplacement evaluation with a finding that he or she is not suited to be an adoptive parent, the individual may petition a court for review of the evaluation.

(b) If the court determines that the petitioner has failed to prove suitability by a preponderance of the evidence, it shall order that the petitioner not be permitted to adopt a minor and shall send a copy of the order to the department to be retained with the copy of the original evaluation. If, at the time of the court's determination, the petitioner has custody of a minor for purposes of adoption, the court shall make an appropriate order for the care and custody of the minor.

(c) If the court determines that the petitioner has proved suitability, the court shall find the petitioner suitable to be an adoptive parent and the petitioner may commence or continue a proceeding for adoption of a minor. The court shall send a copy of its order to the department to be retained with the copy of the original evaluation.

SECTION 2-207. ACTION BY DEPARTMENT.

If, before a decree of adoption is issued, the department learns from an evaluator or another person that a minor has been placed for adoption with an individual who is the subject of a preplacement evaluation on file with the department containing a finding of unsuitability, the department shall immediately review the evaluation and investigate the circumstances of the placement and may request that the individual return the minor to the custody of the person who placed the minor or to the department. If the individual refuses to return the minor, the department shall immediately commence an action or proceeding to remove the minor from the home of the individual pursuant to [the State's child protection statute] and, pending a hearing, the court shall make an appropriate order for the care and custody of the minor.

PART 3. TRANSFER OF PHYSICAL CUSTODY OF MINOR BY HEALTH-CARE FACILITY FOR PURPOSES OF ADOPTION

SECTION 2-301. "HEALTH-CARE FACILITY" DEFINED.

In this [part], "health-care facility" means a hospital, clinic, or other facility authorized by this State to provide services related to birth and neonatal care.

SECTION 2-302. AUTHORIZATION TO TRANSFER PHYSICAL CUSTODY.

(a) A health-care facility shall release a minor for the purpose of adoption to an individual or agency not otherwise legally entitled to the physical custody of the minor if, in the presence of an employee authorized by the health-care facility, the woman who gave birth to the minor signs an authorization of the transfer of physical custody.

(b) An authorized employee in whose presence the authorization required under subsection (a) is signed shall attest the signing in writing.

SECTION 2-303. REPORTS TO DEPARTMENT.

(a) No later than 72 hours after a release pursuant to Section 2-302, a health-care facility that releases a minor for purposes of adoption shall transmit to the department a copy of the authorization required by Section 2-302 and shall report:

(1) the name, address, and telephone number of the person who authorized the release;

(2) the name, address, and telephone number of the person to whom physical custody was transferred; and

(3) the date of the transfer.

(b) No later than 30 days after a release pursuant to Section 2-302, the person to whom physical custody of a minor was transferred shall report to the department which, if any, of the following has occurred:

(1) the filing of a petition for adoption with the name and address of the petitioner;

(2) the acquisition of custody of the minor by an agency and the name and address of the agency;

(3) the return of the minor to a parent or other person having legal custody and the name and address of the parent or other person; or

(4) the transfer of physical custody of the minor to another individual and the name and address of the individual.

SECTION 2-304. ACTION BY DEPARTMENT.

(a) If the department receives a report required under Section 2-303(a) from a health-care facility, but does not receive the report required under Section 2-303(b) within 45 days after the transfer of a minor, the department shall immediately investigate to determine the whereabouts of the minor.

(b) If none of the dispositions listed in Section 2-303(b)(1) through (3) has occurred, or the minor has been transferred to an individual described in Section 2-303(b)(4) who has not filed a petition to adopt, the department shall immediately take appropriate action to remove the minor from the individual to whom the minor has been transferred.

(c) The department may also review and investigate compliance with Sections 2-101 through 2-106 and may maintain an action in the [appropriate] court to compel compliance.

PART 4. CONSENT TO AND RELINQUISHMENT FOR ADOPTION

SECTION 2-401. PERSONS WHOSE CONSENT REQUIRED.

(a) Unless consent is not required or is dispensed with by Section 2-402, in a direct placement of a minor for adoption by a parent or guardian authorized under this [Act] to place the minor, a petition to adopt the minor may be granted only if consent to the adoption has been executed by:

(1) the woman who gave birth to the minor and the man, if any, who:

(i) is or has been married to the woman if the minor was born during the marriage or within 300 days after the marriage was terminated or a court issued a decree of separation;

(ii) attempted to marry the woman before the minor's birth by a marriage solemnized in apparent compliance with law, although the attempted marriage is or could be declared invalid, if the minor was born during the attempted marriage or within 300 days after the attempted marriage was terminated;

(iii) has been judicially determined to be the father of the minor, or has signed a document that has the effect of establishing his parentage of the minor, and:

(A) has provided, in accordance with his financial means, reasonable and consistent payments for the support of the minor and has visited or communicated with the minor; or

(B) after the minor's birth, but before the minor's placement for adoption, has married the woman who gave birth to the minor or attempted to marry her by a marriage solemnized in apparent compliance with law, although the attempted marriage is or could be declared invalid; or

(iv) has received the minor into his home and openly held out the minor as his child;

(2) the minor's guardian if expressly authorized by a court to consent to the minor's adoption; or

(3) the current adoptive or other legally recognized mother and father of the minor.

(b) Unless consent is not required under Section 2-402, in a placement of a minor for adoption by an agency authorized under this [Act] to place the minor, a petition to adopt the minor may be granted only if consent to the adoption has been executed by:

(1) the agency that placed the minor for adoption; and

(2) any individuals described in subsection (a) who have not relinquished the minor.

(c) Unless the court dispenses with the minor's consent, a petition to adopt a minor who has attained 12 years of age may be granted only if, in addition to any consent required by subsections (a) and (b), the minor has executed an informed consent to the adoption.

SECTION 2-402. PERSONS WHOSE CONSENT NOT REQUIRED.

(a) Consent to an adoption of a minor is not required of:

(1) an individual who has relinquished the minor to an agency for purposes of adoption;

(2) an individual whose parental relationship to the minor has been judicially terminated or determined not to exist;

(3) a parent who has been judicially declared incompetent;

(4) a man who has not been married to the woman who gave birth to the minor and who, after the conception of the minor, executes a verified statement denying paternity or disclaiming any interest in the minor and acknowledging that his statement is irrevocable when executed;

(5) the personal representative of a deceased parent's estate; or

(6) a parent or other person who has not executed a consent or a relinquishment and who fails to file an answer or make an appearance in a proceeding for adoption or for termination of a parental relationship within the requisite time after service of notice of the proceeding.

(b) The court may dispense with the consent of:

(1) a guardian or an agency whose consent is otherwise required upon a finding that the consent is being withheld contrary to the best interest of a minor adoptee; or

(2) a minor adoptee who has attained 12 years of age upon a finding that it is not in the best interest of the minor to require the consent.

SECTION 2-403. INDIVIDUALS WHO MAY RELINQUISH MINOR.

A parent or guardian whose consent to the adoption of a minor is required by Section 2-401 may relinquish to an agency all rights with respect to the minor, including legal and physical custody and the right to consent to the minor's adoption.

SECTION 2-404. TIME AND PREREQUISITES FOR EXECUTION OF CONSENT OR RELINQUISHMENT.

(a) A parent whose consent to the adoption of a minor is required by Section 2-401 may execute a consent or a relinquishment only after the minor is born. A parent who executes a consent or relinquishment may revoke the consent or relinquishment within 192 hours after the birth of the minor.

(b) A guardian may execute a consent to the adoption of a minor or a relinquishment at any time after being authorized by a court to do so.

(c) An agency that places a minor for adoption may execute its consent at any time before or during the hearing on the petition for adoption.

(d) A minor adoptee whose consent is required may execute a consent at any time before or during the hearing on the petition for adoption.

(e) Before executing a consent or relinquishment, a parent must have been informed of the meaning and consequences of adoption, the availability of personal and legal counseling, the consequences of misidentifying the other parent, the procedure for releasing information about the health and other characteristics of the parent which may affect the physical or psychological well-being of the adoptee, and the procedure for the consensual release of the parent's identity to an adoptee, an adoptee's direct descendant, or an adoptive parent pursuant to [Article] 6. The parent must have had an opportunity to indicate in a signed document whether and under what circumstances the parent is or is not willing to release identifying information, and must have been informed of the procedure for changing the document at a later time.

SECTION 2-405. PROCEDURE FOR EXECUTION OF CONSENT OR RELINQUISHMENT.

(a) A consent or relinquishment executed by a parent or guardian must be signed or confirmed in the presence of:

(1) a judge of a court of record;

(2) an individual whom a judge of a court of record designates to take consents or relinquishments;

(3) an employee other than an employee of an agency to which a minor is relinquished whom an agency designates to take consents or relinquishments;

(4) a lawyer other than a lawyer who is representing an adoptive parent or the agency to which a minor is relinquished;

(5) a commissioned officer on active duty in the military service of the United States, if the individual executing the consent or relinquishment is in military service; or

(6) an officer of the foreign service or a consular officer of the United States in another country, if the individual executing the consent or relinquishment is in that country.

(b) A consent executed by a minor adoptee must be signed or confirmed in the presence of the court in the proceeding for adoption or in a manner the court directs.

(c) A parent who is a minor is competent to execute a consent or relinquishment if the parent has had access to counseling and has had the advice of a lawyer who is not representing an adoptive parent or the agency to which the parent's child is relinquished.

(d) An individual before whom a consent or relinquishment is signed or confirmed under subsection (a) shall certify in writing that he or she orally explained the contents and consequences of the consent or relinquishment, and to the best of his or her knowledge or belief, the individual executing the consent or relinquishment:

(1) read or was read the consent or relinquishment and understood it;

(2) signed the consent or relinquishment voluntarily and received or was offered a copy of it;

(3) was furnished the information and afforded an opportunity to sign the document described by Section 2-404(e);

(4) received or was offered counseling services and information about adoption; and

(5) if a parent who is a minor, was advised by a lawyer who is not representing an adoptive parent or the agency to which the parent's child is being relinquished, or, if an adult, was informed of the right to have a lawyer who is not representing an adoptive parent or an agency to which the parent's child is being relinquished.

(e) A prospective adoptive parent named or described in a consent to the adoption of a minor shall sign a statement indicating an intention to adopt the minor, acknowledging an obligation to return legal and physical custody of the minor to the minor's parent if the parent revokes the consent within the time specified in Section 2-404(a), and acknowledging responsibility for the minor's support and medical and other care if the consent is not revoked.

(f) If an agency accepts a relinquishment, an employee of the agency shall sign a statement accepting the relinquishment, acknowledging its obligation to return legal and physical custody of the child to the minor's parent if the parent revokes the relinquishment within the time indicated in Section 2-404(a), and acknowledging responsibility for the minor's support and medical and other care if the relinquishment is not revoked.

(g) An individual before whom a consent or a relinquishment is signed or confirmed shall certify having received the statements required by subsections (e) and (f).

(h) A consent by an agency to the adoption of a minor in the agency's legal custody must be executed by the head or an individual authorized by the agency and must be signed or confirmed under oath in the presence of an individual authorized to take acknowledgments.

(i) A consent or relinquishment executed and signed or confirmed in another State or country is valid if in accordance with this [Act] or with the law and procedure prevailing where executed.

SECTION 2-406. CONTENT OF CONSENT OR RELINQUISHMENT.

(a) A consent or relinquishment required from a parent or guardian must be in writing and contain, in plain English or, if the native language of the parent or guardian is a language other than English, in that language:

(1) the date, place, and time of the execution of the consent or relinquishment;

(2) the name, date of birth, and current mailing address of the individual executing the consent or relinquishment;

(3) the date of birth and the name or pseudonym of the minor adoptee;

(4) if a consent, the name, address, and telephone and telecopier numbers of the lawyer representing the prospective adoptive parent with whom the individual executing the consent has placed or intends to place the minor for adoption;

(5) if a relinquishment, the name, address, and telephone and telecopier numbers of the agency to which the minor is being relinquished; and

(6) specific instructions as to how to revoke the consent or relinquishment and how to commence an action to set it aside.

(b) A consent must state that the parent or guardian executing the document is voluntarily and unequivocally consenting to the transfer of legal and physical custody to, and the adoption of the minor by, a specific adoptive parent whom the parent or guardian has selected.

(c) A relinquishment must state that the individual executing the relinquishment voluntarily consents to the permanent transfer of legal and physical custody of the minor to the agency for the purposes of adoption.

(d) A consent or relinquishment must state:

(1) an understanding that after the consent or relinquishment is signed or confirmed in substantial compliance with Section 2-405, it is final and, except under a circumstance stated in Section 2-408 or 2-409, may not be revoked or set aside for any reason, including the failure of an adoptive parent to permit the individual executing the consent or relinquishment to visit or communicate with the minor adoptee;

(2) an understanding that the adoption will extinguish all parental rights and obligations the individual executing the consent or relinquishment has with respect to the minor adoptee, except for arrearages of child support, and will remain valid whether or not any agreement for visitation or communication with the minor adoptee is later performed;

(3) that the individual executing the consent or relinquishment has:

(i) received a copy of the consent or relinquishment;

(ii) received or been offered counseling services and information about adoption which explains the meaning and consequences of an adoption;

(iii) been advised, if a parent who is a minor, by a lawyer who is not representing an adoptive parent or the agency to which the minor adoptee is being relinquished, or, if an adult, has been informed of the right to have a lawyer who is not representing an adoptive parent or the agency;

(iv) been provided the information and afforded an opportunity to sign the document described in Section 2-404(e); and

(v) been advised of the obligation to provide the information required under Section 2-106;

(4) that the individual executing the consent or relinquishment has not received or been promised any money or anything of value for the consent or the relinquishment, except for payments authorized by [Article] 7;

(5) that the minor is not an Indian child as defined in the Indian Child Welfare Act, 25 U.S.C. Sections 1901 et seq.;

(6) that the individual believes the adoption of the minor is in the minor's best interest; and

(7) if a consent, that the individual who is consenting waives further notice unless the adoption is contested, appealed, or denied.

(e) A relinquishment may provide that the individual who is relinquishing waives notice of any proceeding for adoption, or waives notice unless the adoption is contested, appealed, or denied.

(f) A consent or relinquishment may provide for its revocation if:

(1) another consent or relinquishment is not executed within a specified period;

(2) a court decides not to terminate another individual's parental relationship to the minor; or

(3) in a direct placement for adoption, a petition for adoption by a prospective adoptive parent, named or described in the consent, is denied or withdrawn.

SECTION 2-407. CONSEQUENCES OF CONSENT OR RELINQUISHMENT.

(a) Except under a circumstance stated in Section 2-408, a consent to the adoption of a minor which is executed by a parent or guardian in substantial compliance with Sections 2-405 and 2-406 is final and irrevocable, and:

(1) unless a court orders otherwise to protect the welfare of the minor, entitles the prospective adoptive parent named or described in the consent to the legal and physical custody of the minor and imposes on that individual responsibility for the support and medical and other care of the minor;

(2) terminates any duty of a parent who executed the consent with respect to the minor, except for arrearages of child support; and

(3) terminates any right of a parent or guardian who executed the consent to object to the minor's adoption by the prospective adoptive parent and any right to notice of the proceeding for adoption unless the adoption is contested, appealed, or denied.

(b) Except under a circumstance stated in Section 2-409, a relinquishment of a minor to an agency which is executed by a parent or guardian in substantial compliance with Sections 2-405 and 2-406 is final and irrevocable and:

(1) unless a court orders otherwise to protect the welfare of the minor, entitles the agency to the legal custody of the minor until a decree of adoption becomes final;

(2) empowers the agency to place the minor for adoption, consent to the minor's adoption, and delegate to a prospective adoptive parent responsibility for the support and medical and other care of the minor;

(3) terminates any duty of the individual who executed the relinquishment with respect to the minor, except for arrearages of child support; and

(4) terminates any right of the individual who executed the relinquishment to object to the minor's adoption and, unless otherwise provided in the relinquishment, any right to notice of the proceeding for adoption.

SECTION 2-408. REVOCATION OF CONSENT.

(a) In a direct placement of a minor for adoption by a parent or guardian, a consent is revoked if:

(1) within 192 hours after the birth of the minor, a parent who executed the consent notifies in writing the prospective adoptive parent, or the adoptive parent's lawyer, that the parent revokes the consent, or the parent complies with any other instructions for revocation specified in the consent; or

(2) the individual who executed the consent and the prospective adoptive parent named or described in the consent agree to its revocation.

(b) In a direct placement of a minor for adoption by a parent or guardian, the court shall set aside the consent if the individual who executed the consent establishes:

(1) by clear and convincing evidence, before a decree of adoption is issued, that the consent was obtained by fraud or duress;

(2) by a preponderance of the evidence before a decree of adoption is issued that, without good cause shown, a petition to adopt was not filed within 60 days after the minor was placed for adoption; or

(3) by a preponderance of the evidence, that a condition permitting revocation has occurred, as expressly provided for in the consent pursuant to Section 2-406.

(c) If the consent of an individual who had legal and physical custody of a minor when the minor was placed for adoption or when the consent was executed is revoked, the prospective adoptive parent shall immediately return the minor to the individual's custody and move to dismiss a proceeding for adoption or termination of the individual's parental relationship to the minor. If the minor is not returned immediately, the individual may petition the court named in the consent for appropriate relief. The court shall hear the petition expeditiously.

(d) If the consent of an individual who had legal and physical custody of a minor when the minor was placed for adoption or the consent was executed is set aside under subsection (b)(1), the court shall order the return of the minor to the custody of the individual and dismiss a proceeding for adoption.

(e) If the consent of an individual who had legal and physical custody of a minor when the minor was placed for adoption or the consent was executed is set aside under subsection (b)(2) or (3) and no ground exists under [Article] 3, [Part] 5, for terminating the relationship of parent and child between the individual and the minor, the court shall dismiss a proceeding for adoption and order the return of the minor to the custody of the individual unless the court finds that return will be detrimental to the minor.

(f) If the consent of an individual who did not have physical custody of a minor when the minor was placed for adoption or when the consent was executed is revoked or set aside and no ground exists under [Article] 3, [Part] 5, for terminating the relationship of parent and child between the individual and the minor, the court shall dismiss a proceeding for adoption and issue an order providing for the care and custody of the minor according to the best interest of the minor.

SECTION 2-409. REVOCATION OF RELINQUISHMENT.

(a) A relinquishment is revoked if:

(1) within 192 hours after the birth of the minor, a parent who executed the relinquishment gives written notice to the agency that accepted it, that the parent revokes the relinquishment, or the parent complies with any other instructions for revocation specified in the relinquishment; or

(2) the individual who executed the relinquishment and the agency that accepted it agree to its revocation.

(b) The court shall set aside a relinquishment if the individual who executed the relinquishment establishes:

(1) by clear and convincing evidence, before a decree of adoption is issued, that the relinquishment was obtained by fraud or duress; or

(2) by a preponderance of the evidence, that a condition permitting revocation has occurred, as expressly provided for in the relinquishment pursuant to Section 2-406.

(c) If a relinquishment by an individual who had legal and physical custody of a minor when the relinquishment was executed is revoked, the agency shall immediately return the minor to the individual's custody and move to dismiss a proceeding for adoption. If the minor is not returned immediately, the individual may petition the court named in the relinquishment for appropriate relief. The court shall hear the petition expeditiously.

(d) If a relinquishment by an individual who had legal and physical custody of a minor when the relinquishment was executed is set aside under subsection (b)(1), the court shall dismiss a proceeding for adoption and order the return of the minor to the custody of the individual.

(e) If a relinquishment by an individual who had legal and physical custody of a minor when the relinquishment was executed is set aside under subsection (b)(2) and no ground exists under [Article] 3, [Part] 5, for terminating the relationship of parent and child between the individual and the minor, the court shall dismiss a proceeding for adoption and order the return of the minor to the custody of the individual unless the court finds that return will be detrimental to the minor.

(f) If a relinquishment by an individual who did not have physical custody of a minor when the relinquishment was executed is revoked or set aside and no ground exists under [Article] 3, [Part] 5, for terminating the relationship of parent and child between the individual and the minor, the court shall dismiss a proceeding for adoption and shall issue an order providing for the care and custody of the minor according to the best interest of the minor.

ARTICLE 3. GENERAL PROCEDURE FOR ADOPTION OF MINORS

PART 1. JURISDICTION AND VENUE

SECTION 3-101. JURISDICTION.

(a) Except as otherwise provided in subsections (b) and (c), a court of this State has jurisdiction over a proceeding for the adoption of a minor commenced under this [Act] if:

(1) immediately before commencement of the proceeding, the minor lived in this State with a parent, a guardian, a prospective adoptive parent, or another person acting as parent, for at least six consecutive months, excluding periods of temporary absence, or, in the case

of a minor under six months of age, lived in this State from soon after birth with any of those individuals and there is available in this State substantial evidence concerning the minor's present or future care;

(2) immediately before commencement of the proceeding, the prospective adoptive parent lived in this State for at least six consecutive months, excluding periods of temporary absence, and there is available in this State substantial evidence concerning the minor's present or future care;

(3) the agency that placed the minor for adoption is located in this State and it is in the best interest of the minor that a court of this State assume jurisdiction because:

(i) the minor and the minor's parents, or the minor and the prospective adoptive parent, have a significant connection with this State; and

(ii) there is available in this State substantial evidence concerning the minor's present or future care;

(4) the minor and the prospective adoptive parent are physically present in this State and the minor has been abandoned or it is necessary in an emergency to protect the minor because the minor has been subjected to or threatened with mistreatment or abuse or is otherwise neglected; or

(5) it appears that no other State would have jurisdiction under prerequisites substantially in accordance with paragraphs (1) through (4), or another State has declined to exercise jurisdiction on the ground that this State is the more appropriate forum to hear a petition for adoption of the minor, and it is in the best interest of the minor that a court of this State assume jurisdiction.

(b) A court of this State may not exercise jurisdiction over a proceeding for adoption of a minor if at the time the petition for adoption is filed a proceeding concerning the custody or adoption of the minor is pending in a court of another State exercising jurisdiction substantially in conformity with [the Uniform Child Custody Jurisdiction Act] or this [Act] unless the proceeding is stayed by the court of the other State.

(c) If a court of another State has issued a decree or order concerning the custody of a minor who may be the subject of a proceeding for adoption in this State, a court of this State may not exercise jurisdiction over a proceeding for adoption of the minor unless:

(1) the court of this State finds that the court of the State which issued the decree or order:

(i) does not have continuing jurisdiction to modify the decree or order under jurisdictional prerequisites substantially in accordance with [the Uniform Child Custody Jurisdiction Act] or has declined to assume jurisdiction to modify the decree or order; or

(ii) does not have jurisdiction over a proceeding for adoption substantially in conformity with subsection (a)(1) through (4) or has declined to assume jurisdiction over a proceeding for adoption; and

(2) the court of this State has jurisdiction over the proceeding.

SECTION 3-102. VENUE.

A petition for adoption of a minor may be filed in the court in the [county] in which a petitioner lives, the minor lives, or an office of the agency that placed the minor is located.

PART 2. GENERAL PROCEDURAL PROVISIONS

SECTION 3-201. APPOINTMENT OF LAWYER OR GUARDIAN AD LITEM.

(a) In a proceeding under this [Act] which may result in the termination of a relationship of parent and child, the court shall appoint a lawyer for any indigent, minor, or incompetent individual who appears in the proceeding and whose parental relationship to a child may be terminated, unless the court finds that the minor or incompetent individual has sufficient financial means to hire a lawyer, or the indigent individual declines to be represented by a lawyer.

(b) The court shall appoint a guardian ad litem for a minor adoptee in a contested proceeding under this [Act] and may appoint a guardian ad litem for a minor adoptee in an uncontested proceeding.

SECTION 3-202. NO RIGHT TO JURY.

A proceeding under this [Act] for adoption or termination of a parental relationship must be heard by the court without a jury.

SECTION 3-203. CONFIDENTIALITY OF PROCEEDINGS.

Except for a proceeding pursuant to [Article] 7, a civil proceeding under this [Act] must be heard in closed court.

SECTION 3-204. CUSTODY DURING PENDENCY OF PROCEEDING.

In order to protect the welfare of the minor, the court shall make an interim order for custody of a minor adoptee according to the best interest of the minor in a contested proceeding under this [Act] for adoption or termination of a parental relationship and may make an interim order for custody in an uncontested proceeding.

SECTION 3-205. REMOVAL OF ADOPTEE FROM STATE.

Before a decree of adoption is issued, a petitioner may not remove a minor adoptee for more than 30 consecutive days from the State in which the petitioner resides without the permission of the court, if the minor was placed directly for adoption, or, if an agency placed the minor for adoption, the permission of the agency.

PART 3. PETITION FOR ADOPTION OF MINOR

SECTION 3-301. STANDING TO PETITION TO ADOPT.

(a) Except as otherwise provided in subsection (c), the only individuals who have standing to petition to adopt a minor under this [article] are:

(1) an individual with whom a minor has been placed for adoption or who has been selected as a prospective adoptive parent by a person authorized under this [Act] to place the minor for adoption; or

(2) an individual with whom a minor has not been placed for adoption or who has not been selected or rejected as a prospective adoptive parent pursuant to [Article] 2, [Parts] 1 through 3, but who has had physical custody of the minor for at least six months immediately before seeking to file a petition for adoption and is allowed to file the petition by the court for good cause shown.

(b) The spouse of a petitioner must join in the petition unless legally separated from the petitioner or judicially declared incompetent.

(c) A petition for adoption of a minor stepchild by a stepparent may be filed under [Article] 4 and a petition for adoption of an emancipated minor may be filed under [Article] 5.

SECTION 3-302. TIME FOR FILING PETITION.

Unless the court allows a later filing, a prospective adoptive parent with standing under Section 3-301(a)(1) shall file a petition for adoption no later than 30 days after a minor is placed for adoption with that individual.

SECTION 3-303. CAPTION OF PETITION.

The caption of a petition for adoption of a minor must contain the name of or a pseudonym for the minor adoptee. The caption may not contain the name of the petitioner.

SECTION 3-304. CONTENT OF PETITION.

(a) A petition for adoption of a minor must be signed and verified by the petitioner and contain the following information or state why any of the information omitted is not contained in the petition:

(1) the full name, age, and place and duration of residence of the petitioner;

(2) the current marital status of the petitioner, including the date and place of any marriage, the date of any legal separation or divorce, and the date of any judicial determination that a petitioner's spouse is incompetent;

(3) that the petitioner has facilities and resources to provide for the care and support of the minor;

(4) that a preplacement evaluation containing a finding that the petitioner is suited to be an adoptive parent has been prepared or updated within the 18 months next preceding the placement, or that the absence of a preplacement evaluation has been excused by a court for good cause shown or is not required under Section 2-201;

(5) the first name, sex, and date, or approximate date, and place of birth of the minor adoptee and a statement that the minor is or is not an Indian child as defined in the Indian Child Welfare Act, 25 U.S.C. Sections 1901 et seq.;

(6) the circumstances under which the petitioner obtained physical custody of the minor, including the date of placement of the minor with the petitioner for adoption and the name of the agency or the name or relationship to the minor of the individual that placed the minor;

(7) the length of time the minor has been in the custody of the petitioner and, if the minor is not in the physical custody of the petitioner, the reason why the petitioner does not have custody and the date and manner in which the petitioner intends to obtain custody;

(8) a description and estimate of the value of any property of the minor;

(9) that any law governing interstate or intercountry placement was complied with;

(10) the name or relationship to the minor of any individual who has executed a consent or relinquishment to the adoption or a disclaimer of paternal interest, and the name or relationship to the minor of any individual whose consent or relinquishment may be required, but whose parental relationship has not been terminated, and any fact or circumstance that may excuse the lack of consent;

(11) that a previous petition by the petitioner to adopt has or has not been made in any court, and its disposition; and

(12) a description of any previous court order or pending proceeding known to the petitioner concerning custody of or visitation with the minor and any other fact known to the petitioner and needed to establish the jurisdiction of the court.

(b) The petitioner shall request in the petition:

(1) that the petitioner be permitted to adopt the minor as the petitioner's child;

(2) that the court approve the full name by which the minor is to be known if the petition is granted; and

(3) any other relief sought by the petitioner.

SECTION 3-305. REQUIRED DOCUMENTS.

(a) Before the hearing on a petition for adoption, the following must be filed:

(1) a certified copy of the birth certificate or other record of the date and place of birth of the minor adoptee;

(2) any consent, relinquishment, or disclaimer of paternal interest with respect to the minor that has been executed, and any written certifications required by Section 2-405(d) and (g) from the individual before whom a consent or relinquishment was executed;

(3) a certified copy of any court order terminating the rights and duties of the minor's parents or guardian;

(4) a certified copy of each parent's or former parent's marriage certificate, decree of divorce, annulment, or dissolution, or agreement or decree of legal separation, and a certified copy of any court order determining the parent's or former parent's incompetence;

(5) a certified copy of any existing court order or the petition in any pending proceeding concerning custody of or visitation with the minor;

(6) a copy of the preplacement evaluation and of the evaluation during the pendency of the proceeding for adoption;

(7) a copy of any report containing the information required by Section 2-106;

(8) a document signed pursuant to Section 2-404(e);

(9) a certified copy of the petitioner's marriage certificate, decree of divorce, annulment, or dissolution, or agreement or decree of legal separation, and a certified copy of any court order determining the incompetence of the petitioner's spouse;

(10) a copy of any agreement with a public agency to provide a subsidy for the benefit of a minor adoptee with a special need;

(11) if an agency placed the minor adoptee, a verified document from the agency stating:

(i) the circumstances under which it obtained custody of the minor for purposes of adoption;

(ii) that it complied with any provision of law governing an interstate or intercountry placement of the minor;

(iii) the name or relationship to the minor of any individual whose consent is required, but who has not executed a consent or a relinquishment or whose parental relationship has not been terminated, and any fact or circumstance that may excuse the lack of consent or relinquishment; and

(iv) whether it has executed its consent to the proposed adoption and whether it waives notice of the proceeding; and

(12) the name and address, if known, of any person who is entitled to receive notice of the proceeding for adoption.

(b) If an item required by subsection (a) is not available, the person responsible for furnishing the item shall file an affidavit explaining its absence.

PART 4. NOTICE OF PENDENCY OF PROCEEDING

SECTION 3-401. SERVICE OF NOTICE.

(a) Unless notice has been waived, notice of a proceeding for adoption of a minor must be served, within 20 days after a petition for adoption is filed, upon:

(1) an individual whose consent to the adoption is required under Section 2-401, but notice need not be served upon an individual whose parental relationship to the minor or whose status as a guardian has been terminated;

(2) an agency whose consent to the adoption is required under Section 2-401;

(3) an individual whom the petitioner knows is claiming to be or who is named as the father or possible father of the minor adoptee and whose paternity of the minor has not been judicially determined, but notice need not be served upon a man who has executed a verified statement, as described in Section 2-402(a)(4), denying paternity or disclaiming any interest in the minor;

(4) an individual other than the petitioner who has legal or physical custody of the minor adoptee or who has a right of visitation with the minor under an existing court order issued by a court in this or another State;

(5) the spouse of the petitioner if the spouse has not joined in the petition; and

(6) a grandparent of a minor adoptee if the grandparent's child is a deceased parent of the minor and, before death, the deceased parent had not executed a consent or relinquishment or the deceased parent's parental relationship to the minor had not been terminated.

(b) The court shall require notice of a proceeding for adoption of a minor to be served upon any person the court finds, at any time during the proceeding, is:

(1) a person described in subsection (a) who has not been given notice;

(2) an individual who has revoked a consent or relinquishment pursuant to Section 2-408(a) or 2-409(a) or is attempting to have a consent or relinquishment set aside pursuant to Section 2-408(b) or 2-409(b); or

(3) a person who, on the basis of a previous relationship with the minor adoptee, a parent, an alleged parent, or the petitioner, can provide information that is relevant to the proposed adoption and that the court in its discretion wants to hear.

SECTION 3-402. CONTENT OF NOTICE.

A notice required by Section 3-401 must use a pseudonym for a petitioner or any individual named in the petition for adoption who has not waived confidentiality and must contain:

(1) the caption of the petition;

(2) the address and telephone number of the court where the petition is pending;

(3) a concise summary of the relief requested in the petition;

(4) the name, mailing address, and telephone number of the petitioner or petitioner's lawyer;

(5) a conspicuous statement of the method of responding to the notice of the proceeding for adoption and the consequences of failure to respond; and

(6) any statement required by [other applicable law or rule].

SECTION 3-403. MANNER AND EFFECT OF SERVICE.

(a) Personal service of the notice required by Section 3-401 must be made in a manner appropriate under [the rules of civil procedure for the service of process in a civil action in this State] unless the court otherwise directs.

(b) Except as otherwise provided in subsection (c), a person who fails to respond to the notice within 20 days after its service may not appear in or receive further notice of the proceeding for adoption.

(c) An individual who is a respondent in a petition to terminate the relationship of parent and child pursuant to [Part] 5 which is served upon the individual with the notice required by Section 3-401 may not appear in or receive further notice of the proceeding for adoption or for termination unless the individual responds to the notice as required by Section 3-504.

SECTION 3-404. INVESTIGATION AND NOTICE TO UNKNOWN FATHER.

(a) If, at any time in a proceeding for adoption or for termination of a relationship of parent and child under [Part] 5, the court finds that an unknown father of a minor adoptee may not have received notice, the court shall determine whether he can be identified. The determination must be based on evidence that includes inquiry of appropriate persons in an effort to identify an unknown father for the purpose of providing notice.

(b) The inquiry required by subsection (a) must include whether:

(1) the woman who gave birth to the minor adoptee was married at the probable time of conception of the minor, or at a later time;

(2) the woman was cohabiting with a man at the probable time of conception of the minor;

(3) the woman has received payments or promises of support, other than from a governmental agency, with respect to the minor or because of her pregnancy;

(4) the woman has named any individual as the father on the birth certificate of the minor or in connection with applying for or receiving public assistance; and

(5) any individual has formally or informally acknowledged or claimed paternity of the minor in a jurisdiction in which the woman resided during or since her pregnancy, or in which the minor has resided or resides, at the time of the inquiry.

(c) If inquiry pursuant to subsection (b) identifies as the father of the minor an individual who has not received notice of the proceeding, the court shall require notice to be served upon him pursuant to Section 3-403 unless service is not possible because his whereabouts are unknown.

(d) If, after inquiry pursuant to subsection (b), the court finds that personal service cannot be made upon the father of the minor because his identity or whereabouts is unknown, the court shall order publication or public posting of the notice only if, on the basis of all information available, the court determines that publication or posting is likely to lead to receipt of notice by the father. If the court determines that publication or posting is not likely to lead to receipt of notice, the court may dispense with the publication or posting of a notice.

(e) If, in an inquiry pursuant to this section, the woman who gave birth to the minor adoptee fails to disclose the identity of a possible father or reveal his whereabouts, she must be advised that the proceeding for adoption may be delayed or subject to challenge if a possible father is not given notice of the proceeding, that the lack of information about the father's medical and genetic history may be detrimental to the adoptee, and that she is subject to a civil penalty if she knowingly misidentified the father.

SECTION 3-405. WAIVER OF NOTICE.

(a) A person entitled to receive notice required under this [Act] may waive the notice before the court or in a consent, relinquishment, or other document signed by the person.

(b) Except for the purpose of moving to revoke a consent or relinquishment on the ground that it was obtained by fraud or duress, a person who has waived notice may not appear in the proceeding for adoption.

PART 5. PETITION TO TERMINATE RELATIONSHIP BETWEEN PARENT AND CHILD

SECTION 3-501. AUTHORIZATION.

A petition to terminate the relationship between a parent or an alleged parent and a minor child may be filed in a proceeding for adoption under this [Act] by:

(1) a parent or a guardian who has selected a prospective adoptive parent for a minor and who intends to place, or has placed, the minor with that individual;

(2) a parent whose spouse has filed a petition under [Article] 4 to adopt the parent's minor child;

(3) a prospective adoptive parent of the minor who has filed a petition to adopt under this [article] or [Article] 4; or

(4) an agency that has selected a prospective adoptive parent for the minor and intends to place, or has placed, the minor with that individual.

SECTION 3-502. TIMING AND CONTENT OF PETITION.

(a) A petition under this [part] may be filed at any time after a petition for adoption has been filed under this [article] or [Article] 4 and before entry of a decree of adoption.

(b) A petition under this [part] must be signed and verified by the petitioner, be filed with the court, and state:

(1) the name or pseudonym of the petitioner;

(2) the name of the minor;

(3) the name and last known address of the parent or alleged parent whose parental relationship to the minor is to be terminated;

(4) the facts and circumstances forming the basis for the petition and the grounds on which termination of a parental relationship is sought;

(5) if the petitioner is a prospective adoptive parent, that the petitioner intends to proceed with the petition to adopt the minor if the petition to terminate is granted; and

(6) if the petitioner is a parent, a guardian, or an agency, that the petitioner has selected the prospective adoptive parent who is the petitioner in the proceeding for adoption.

SECTION 3-503. SERVICE OF PETITION AND NOTICE.

(a) A petition to terminate under this [part] and a notice of hearing on the petition must be served upon the respondent, with notice of the proceeding for adoption, in the manner prescribed in Sections 3-403 and 3-404.

(b) The notice of a hearing must inform the respondent of the method for responding and that:

(1) the respondent has a right to be represented by a lawyer and may be entitled to have a lawyer appointed by the court; and

(2) failure to respond within 20 days after service and, in the case of an alleged father, failure to file a claim of paternity within 20 days after service unless a claim of paternity is pending, will result in termination of the relationship of parent and child between the respondent and the minor unless the proceeding for adoption is dismissed.

SECTION 3-504. GROUNDS FOR TERMINATING RELATIONSHIP.

(a) If the respondent is served with a petition to terminate under this [part] and the accompanying notice and does not respond and, in the case of an alleged father, file a claim of paternity within 20 days after the service unless a claim of paternity is pending, the court shall order the termination of any relationship of parent and child between the respondent and the minor unless the proceeding for adoption is dismissed.

(b) If, under Section 3-404, the court dispenses with service of the petition upon the respondent, the court shall order the termination of any relationship of parent and child between the respondent and the minor unless the proceeding for adoption is dismissed.

(c) If the respondent responds and asserts parental rights, the court shall proceed with the hearing expeditiously. If the court finds, upon clear and convincing evidence, that one of the following grounds exists, and, by a preponderance of the evidence, that termination is in the best interest of the minor, the court shall terminate any relationship of parent and child between the respondent and the minor:

(1) in the case of a minor who has not attained six months of age at the time the petition for adoption is filed, unless the respondent proves by a preponderance of the evidence a compelling reason for not complying with this paragraph, the respondent has failed to:

(i) pay reasonable prenatal, natal, and postnatal expenses in accordance with the respondent's financial means;

(ii) make reasonable and consistent payments, in accordance with the respondent's financial means, for the support of the minor;

(iii) visit regularly with the minor; and

(iv) manifest an ability and willingness to assume legal and physical custody of the minor, if, during this time, the minor was not in the physical custody of the other parent;

(2) in the case of a minor who has attained six months of age at the time a petition for adoption is filed, unless the respondent proves by a preponderance of the evidence a compelling reason for not complying with this paragraph, the respondent, for a period of at least six consecutive months immediately preceding the filing of the petition, has failed to:

(i) make reasonable and consistent payments, in accordance with the respondent's means, for the support of the minor;

(ii) communicate or visit regularly with the minor; and

(iii) manifest an ability and willingness to assume legal and physical custody of the minor, if, during this time, the minor was not in the physical custody of the other parent;

(3) the respondent has been convicted of a crime of violence or of violating a restraining or protective order, and the facts of the crime or violation and the respondent's behavior indicate that the respondent is unfit to maintain a relationship of parent and child with the minor;

(4) the respondent is a man who was not married to the minor's mother when the minor was conceived or born and is not the genetic or adoptive father of the minor; or

(5) termination is justified on a ground specified in [the State's statute for involuntary termination of parental rights].

(d) If the respondent proves by a preponderance of the evidence that he or she had a compelling reason for not complying with subsection (c)(1) or (2) and termination is not justified on a ground stated in subsection (c)(3) through (5), the court may terminate the relationship of parent and child between the respondent and a minor only if it finds, upon clear and convincing evidence, that one of the following grounds exists, and, by a preponderance of the evidence, that termination is in the best interest of the minor:

(1) if the minor is not in the legal and physical custody of the other parent, the respondent is not able or willing promptly to assume legal and physical custody of the minor, and to pay for the minor's support, in accordance with the respondent's financial means;

(2) if the minor is in the legal and physical custody of the other parent and a stepparent, and the stepparent is the prospective adoptive parent, the respondent is not able or willing promptly to establish and maintain contact with the minor and to pay for the minor's support, in accordance with the respondent's financial means;

(3) placing the minor in the respondent's legal and physical custody would pose a risk of substantial harm to the physical or psychological well-being of the minor because the circumstances of the minor's conception, the respondent's behavior during the mother's pregnancy or since the minor's birth, or the respondent's behavior with respect to other minors, indicates that the respondent is unfit to maintain a relationship of parent and child with the minor; or

(4) failure to terminate the relationship of parent and child would be detrimental to the minor.

(e) In making a determination under subsection (d)(4), the court shall consider any relevant factor, including the respondent's efforts to obtain or maintain legal and physical custody of the minor, the role of other persons in thwarting the respondent's efforts to assert parental rights, the respondent's ability to care for the minor, the age of the minor, the quality of any previous relationship between the respondent and the minor and between the respondent and any other minor children, the duration and suitability of the minor's present custodial environment, and the effect of a change of physical custody on the minor.

SECTION 3-505. EFFECT OF ORDER GRANTING PETITION.

An order issued under this [part] granting the petition:

(1) terminates the relationship of parent and child between the respondent and the minor, except an obligation for arrearages of child support;

(2) extinguishes any right the respondent had to withhold consent to a proposed adoption of the minor or to further notice of a proceeding for adoption; and

(3) is a final order for purposes of appeal.

SECTION 3-506. EFFECT OF ORDER DENYING PETITION.

(a) If the court denies the petition to terminate a relationship of parent and child, the court shall dismiss the proceeding for adoption and shall determine the legal and physical custody of the minor according to the criteria stated in Section 3-704.

(b) An order issued under this [part] denying a petition to terminate a relationship of parent and child is a final order for purposes of appeal.

PART 6. EVALUATION OF ADOPTEE AND PROSPECTIVE ADOPTIVE PARENT

SECTION 3-601. EVALUATION DURING PROCEEDING FOR ADOPTION.

(a) After a petition for adoption of a minor is filed, the court shall order that an evaluation be made by an individual qualified under Section 2-202.

(b) The court shall provide the evaluator with copies of the petition for adoption and of the items filed with the petition.

SECTION 3-602. CONTENT OF EVALUATION.

(a) An evaluation must be based on a personal interview with the petitioner in the petitioner's residence and observation of the relationship between the minor adoptee and the petitioner.

(b) An evaluation must be in writing and contain:

(1) an account of any change in the petitioner's marital status or family history, physical or mental health, home environment,

property, income, or financial obligations since the filing of the pre-placement evaluation;

(2) all reasonably available information concerning the physical, mental, and emotional condition of the minor adoptee which is not included in any report on the minor's health, genetic, and social history filed in the proceeding for adoption;

(3) copies of any court order, judgment, decree, or pending legal proceeding affecting the minor adoptee, the petitioner, or any child of the petitioner;

(4) a list of the expenses, fees, or other charges incurred, paid, or to be paid, and anything of value exchanged or to be exchanged, in connection with the adoption;

(5) any behavior or characteristics of the petitioner which raise a specific concern, as described in Section 2-204(a), about the petitioner or the petitioner's home; and

(6) a finding by the evaluator concerning the suitability of the petitioner and the petitioner's home for the minor adoptee and a recommendation concerning the granting of the petition for adoption.

SECTION 3-603. TIME AND FILING OF EVALUATION.

(a) The evaluator shall complete a written evaluation and file it with the court within 60 days after receipt of the court's order for an evaluation, unless the court for good cause allows a later filing.

(b) If an evaluation produces a specific concern, as described in Section 2-204(a), the evaluation must be filed immediately, and must explain why the concern poses a significant risk of harm to the physical or psychological well-being of the minor.

(c) An evaluator shall give the petitioner a copy of an evaluation when filed with the court and for two years shall retain a copy and a list of every source for each item of information in the evaluation.

PART 7. DISPOSITIONAL HEARING; DECREE OF ADOPTION

SECTION 3-701. TIME FOR HEARING ON PETITION.

The court shall set a date and time for hearing the petition, which must be no sooner than 90 days and no later than 180 days after the petition for adoption has been filed, unless the court for good cause sets an earlier or later date and time.

SECTION 3-702. DISCLOSURE OF FEES AND CHARGES.

At least 10 days before the hearing:

(1) the petitioner shall file with the court a signed and verified accounting of any payment or disbursement of money or anything of value made or agreed to be made by or on behalf of the petitioner in connection with the adoption, or pursuant to [Article] 7. The accounting must include the date and amount of each payment or disbursement made, the name and address of each recipient, and the purpose of each payment or disbursement;

(2) the lawyer for a petitioner shall file with the court an affidavit itemizing any fee, compensation, or other thing of value received by, or agreed to be paid to, the lawyer incidental to the placement and adoption of the minor;

(3) the lawyer for each parent of the minor or for the guardian of the minor shall file with the court an affidavit itemizing any fee, compensation, or other thing of value received by, or agreed to be paid to, the lawyer incidental to the placement and adoption of the minor;

(4) if an agency placed the minor for adoption, the agency shall file with the court an affidavit itemizing any fee, compensation, or other thing of value received by the agency for, or incidental to, the placement and adoption of the minor; and

(5) if a guardian placed the minor for adoption, the guardian shall file with the court an affidavit itemizing any fee, compensation, or other thing of value received by the guardian for, or incidental to, the placement and adoption of the minor.

SECTION 3-703. GRANTING PETITION FOR ADOPTION.

(a) The court shall grant a petition for adoption if it determines that the adoption will be in the best interest of the minor, and that:

(1) at least 90 days have elapsed since the filing of the petition for adoption unless the court for good cause shown waives this requirement;

(2) the adoptee has been in the physical custody of the petitioner for at least 90 days unless the court for good cause shown waives this requirement;

(3) notice of the proceeding for adoption has been served or dispensed with as to any person entitled to receive notice under [Part] 4;

(4) every necessary consent, relinquishment, waiver, disclaimer of paternal interest, or judicial order terminating parental rights, including an order issued under [Part] 5, has been obtained and filed with the court;

(5) any evaluation required by this [Act] has been filed with and considered by the court;

(6) the petitioner is a suitable adoptive parent for the minor;

(7) if applicable, any requirement of this [Act] governing an interstate or intercountry placement for adoption has been met;

(8) the Indian Child Welfare Act, 25 U.S.C. Sections 1901 et seq., is not applicable to the proceeding or, if applicable, its requirements have been met;

(9) an accounting and affidavit required by Section 3-702 have been reviewed by the court, and the court has denied, modified, or ordered reimbursement of any payment or disbursement that is not authorized by [Article] 7 or is unreasonable or unnecessary when compared with the expenses customarily incurred in connection with an adoption;

(10) the petitioner has received each report required by Section 2-106; and

(11) any document signed pursuant to Section 2-404(e) concerning the release of a former parent's identity to the adoptee after the adoptee attains 18 years of age has been filed with the court.

(b) Notwithstanding a finding by the court that an activity prohibited by this [Act] has occurred, if the court makes the determinations required by subsection (a), the court shall grant the petition for adoption and report the violation to the appropriate authorities.

(c) Except as otherwise provided in [Article] 4, the court shall inform the petitioner and any other individual affected by an existing order for visitation or communication with the minor adoptee that the decree of adoption terminates any existing order for visitation or communication.

SECTION 3-704. DENIAL OF PETITION FOR ADOPTION.

If a court denies a petition for adoption, it shall dismiss the proceeding and issue an appropriate order for the legal and physical custody of the minor. If the reason for the denial is that a consent or relinquishment is revoked or set aside pursuant to Section 2-408 or 2-409, the court shall determine the minor's custody according to the criteria stated in those sections. If the petition for adoption is denied for any other reason, the court shall determine the minor's custody according to the best interest of the minor.

SECTION 3-705. DECREE OF ADOPTION.

(a) A decree of adoption must state or contain:

(1) the original name of the minor adoptee, if the adoption is by a stepparent or relative and, in all other adoptions, the original name or a pseudonym;

(2) the name of the petitioner for adoption;

(3) whether the petitioner is married or unmarried;

(4) whether the petitioner is a stepparent of the adoptee;

(5) the name by which the adoptee is to be known and when the name takes effect;

(6) information to be incorporated into a new birth certificate to be issued by the [State Registrar of Vital Records], unless the petitioner or an adoptee who has attained 12 years of age requests that a new certificate not be issued;

(7) the adoptee's date and place of birth, if known, or in the case of an adoptee born outside the United States, as determined pursuant to subsection (b);

(8) the effect of the decree of adoption as stated in Sections 1-104 through 1-106; and

(9) that the adoption is in the best interest of the adoptee.

(b) In determining the date and place of birth of an adoptee born outside the United States, the court shall:

(1) enter the date and place of birth as stated in the birth certificate from the country of origin, the United States Department of State's report of birth abroad, or the documents of the United States Immigration and Naturalization Service;

(2) if the exact place of birth is unknown, enter the information that is known and designate a place of birth according to the best information known with respect to the country of origin;

(3) if the exact date of birth is unknown, determine a date of birth based upon medical evidence as to the probable age of the adoptee and other evidence the court considers appropriate; and

(4) if documents described in paragraph (1) are not available, determine the date and place of birth based upon evidence the court finds appropriate to consider.

(c) Unless a petitioner requests otherwise and the former parent agrees, the decree of adoption may not name a former parent of the adoptee.

(d) Except for a decree of adoption of a minor by a stepparent which is issued pursuant to [Article] 4, a decree of adoption of a minor must contain a statement that the adoption terminates any order for visitation or communication with the minor that was in effect before the decree is issued.

(e) A decree that substantially complies with the requirements of this section is not subject to challenge solely because one or more items required by this section are not contained in the decree.

SECTION 3-706. FINALITY OF DECREE.

A decree of adoption is a final order for purposes of appeal when it is issued and becomes final for other purposes upon the expiration of the time for filing an appeal, if no appeal is filed, or upon the denial or dismissal of any appeal filed within the requisite time.

SECTION 3-707. CHALLENGES TO DECREE.

(a) An appeal from a decree of adoption or other appealable order issued under this [Act] must be heard expeditiously.

(b) A decree or order issued under this [Act] may not be vacated or annulled upon application of a person who waived notice, or who was properly served with notice pursuant to this [Act] and failed to respond or appear, file an answer, or file a claim of paternity within the time allowed.

(c) The validity of a decree of adoption issued under this [Act] may not be challenged for failure to comply with an agreement for visitation or communication with an adoptee.

(d) A decree of adoption or other order issued under this [Act] is not subject to a challenge begun more than six months after the decree or order is issued. If a challenge is brought by an individual whose parental relationship to an adoptee is terminated by a decree or order under this [Act], the court shall deny the challenge, unless the court finds by clear and convincing evidence that the decree or order is not in the best interest of the adoptee.

PART 8. BIRTH CERTIFICATE

SECTION 3-801. REPORT OF ADOPTION.

(a) Within 30 days after a decree of adoption becomes final, the clerk of the court shall prepare a report of adoption on a form furnished by the [State Registrar of Vital Records] and certify and send the report to the [Registrar]. The report must include:

(1) information in the court's record of the proceeding for adoption which is necessary to locate and identify the adoptee's birth certificate or, in the case of an adoptee born outside the United States, evidence the court finds appropriate to consider as to the adoptee's date and place of birth;

(2) information in the court's record of the proceeding for adoption which is necessary to issue a new birth certificate for the adoptee and a request that a new certificate be issued, unless the court, the adoptive parent, or an adoptee who has attained 12 years of age requests that a new certificate not be issued; and

(3) the file number of the decree of adoption and the date on which the decree became final.

(b) Within 30 days after a decree of adoption is amended or vacated, the clerk of the court shall prepare a report of that action on a form furnished by the [Registrar] and shall certify and send the report to the [Registrar]. The report must include information necessary to identify the original report of adoption, and shall also include information necessary to amend or withdraw any new birth certificate that was issued pursuant to the original report of adoption.

SECTION 3-802. ISSUANCE OF NEW BIRTH CERTIFICATE.

(a) Except as otherwise provided in subsection (d), upon receipt of a report of adoption prepared pursuant to Section 3-801, a report of adoption prepared in accordance with the law of another State or country, a certified copy of a decree of adoption together with information necessary to identify the adoptee's original birth certificate and to issue a new certificate, or a report of an amended adoption, the [Registrar] shall:

(1) issue a new birth certificate for an adoptee born in this State and furnish a certified copy of the new certificate to the adoptive parent and to an adoptee who has attained 12 years of age;

(2) forward a certified copy of a report of adoption for an adoptee born in another State to the [Registrar] of the State of birth;

(3) issue a certificate of foreign birth for an adoptee adopted in this State and who was born outside the United States and was not a citizen of the United States at the time of birth, and furnish a certified copy of the certificate to the adoptive parent and to an adoptee who has attained 12 years of age;

(4) notify an adoptive parent of the procedure for obtaining a revised birth certificate through the United States Department of State for an adoptee born outside the United States who was a citizen of the United States at the time of birth; or

(5) in the case of an amended decree of adoption, issue an amended birth certificate according to the procedure in paragraph (1) or (3) or follow the procedure in paragraph (2) or (4).

(b) Unless otherwise specified by the court, a new birth certificate issued pursuant to subsection (a)(1) or (3) or an amended certificate issued pursuant to subsection (a)(5) must include the date and place of birth of the adoptee, substitute the name of the adoptive parent for the name of the individual listed as the adoptee's parent on the original birth certificate, and contain any other information prescribed by [the State's vital records law or regulations].

(c) The [Registrar] shall substitute the new or amended birth certificate for the original birth certificate in the [Registrar's] files. The original certificate and all copies of the certificate in the files of the [Registrar] or any other custodian of vital records in the State must be sealed and are not subject to inspection until 99 years after the adoptee's date of birth, but may be inspected as provided in this [Act].

(d) If the court, the adoptive parent, or an adoptee who has attained 12 years of age requests that a new or amended birth certificate not be issued, the [Registrar] may not issue a new or amended certificate for an adoptee pursuant to subsection (a), but shall forward a certified copy of the report of adoption or of an amended decree of adoption for an adoptee who was born in another State to the appropriate office in the adoptee's State of birth.

(e) Upon receipt of a report that an adoption has been vacated, the [Registrar] shall:

(1) restore the original birth certificate for an individual born in this State to its place in the files, seal any new or amended birth certificate issued pursuant to subsection (a), and not allow inspection of a sealed certificate except upon court order or as otherwise provided in this [Act];

(2) forward the report with respect to an individual born in another State to the appropriate office in the State of birth; or

(3) notify the individual who is granted legal custody of a former adoptee after an adoption is vacated of the procedure for obtaining an original birth certificate through the United States Department of State for a former adoptee born outside the United States who was a citizen of the United States at the time of birth.

(f) Upon request by an individual who was listed as a parent on a child's original birth certificate and who furnishes appropriate proof of the individual's identity, the [Registrar] shall give the individual a noncertified copy of the original birth certificate.

ARTICLE 4. ADOPTION OF MINOR STEPCHILD BY STEPPARENT

SECTION 4-101. OTHER PROVISIONS APPLICABLE TO ADOPTION OF STEPCHILD.

Except as otherwise provided by this [article], [Article] 3 applies to an adoption of a minor stepchild by a stepparent.

SECTION 4-102. STANDING TO ADOPT MINOR STEPCHILD.

(a) A stepparent has standing under this [article] to petition to adopt a minor stepchild who is the child of the stepparent's spouse if:

(1) the spouse has sole legal and physical custody of the child and the child has been in the physical custody of the spouse and the stepparent during the 60 days next preceding the filing of a petition for adoption;

(2) the spouse has joint legal custody of the child with the child's other parent and the child has resided primarily with the spouse and the stepparent during the 12 months next preceding the filing of the petition;

(3) the spouse is deceased or mentally incompetent, but before dying or being judicially declared mentally incompetent, had legal and physical custody of the child, and the child has resided primarily with the stepparent during the 12 months next preceding the filing of the petition; or

(4) an agency placed the child with the stepparent pursuant to Section 2-104.

(b) For good cause shown, a court may allow an individual who does not meet the requirements of subsection (a), but has the consent of the custodial parent of a minor to file a petition for adoption under this [article].

A petition allowed under this subsection must be treated as if the petitioner were a stepparent.

(c) A petition for adoption by a stepparent may be joined with a petition under [Article] 3, [Part] 5, to terminate the relationship of parent and child between a minor adoptee and the adoptee's parent who is not the stepparent's spouse.

SECTION 4-103. LEGAL CONSEQUENCES OF ADOPTION OF STEPCHILD.

(a) Except as otherwise provided in subsections (b) and (c), the legal consequences of an adoption of a stepchild by a stepparent are the same as under Sections 1-103 through 1-106.

(b) An adoption by a stepparent does not affect:

(1) the relationship between the adoptee and the adoptee's parent who is the adoptive stepparent's spouse or deceased spouse;

(2) an existing court order for visitation or communication with a minor adoptee by an individual related to the adoptee through the parent who is the adoptive stepparent's spouse or deceased spouse;

(3) the right of the adoptee or a descendant of the adoptee to inheritance or intestate succession through or from the adoptee's former parent; or

(4) A court order or agreement for visitation or communication with a minor adoptee which is approved by the court pursuant to Section 4-113.

(c) Failure to comply with an agreement or order is not a ground for challenging the validity of an adoption by a stepparent.

SECTION 4-104. CONSENT TO ADOPTION.

Unless consent is not required under Section 2-402, a petition to adopt a minor stepchild may be granted only if consent to the adoption has been executed by a stepchild who has attained 12 years of age; and

(1) the minor's parents as described in Section 2-401(a);

(2) the minor's guardian if expressly authorized by a court to consent to the minor's adoption; or

(3) an agency that placed the minor for adoption by the stepparent.

SECTION 4-105. CONTENT OF CONSENT BY STEPPARENT'S SPOUSE.

(a) A consent executed by a parent who is the stepparent's spouse must be signed or confirmed in the presence of an individual specified in Section 2-405, or an individual authorized to take acknowledgements.

(b) A consent under subsection (a) must be in writing, must contain the required statements described in Section 2-406 (a)(1) through (3) and (d)(3) through (6), may contain the optional statements described in Section 2-406(f), and must state that:

(1) the parent executing the consent has legal and physical custody of the parent's minor child and voluntarily and unequivocally consents to the adoption of the minor by the stepparent;

(2) the adoption will not terminate the parental relationship between the parent executing the consent and the minor child; and

(3) the parent executing the consent understands and agrees that the adoption will terminate the relationship of parent and child between the minor's other parent and the minor, and will terminate any existing court order for custody, visitation, or communication with the minor, but:

(i) the minor and any descendant of the minor will retain rights of inheritance from or through the minor's other parent;

(ii) a court order for visitation or communication with the minor by an individual related to the minor through the parent executing the consent, or an agreement or order concerning another individual which is approved by the court pursuant to Section 4-113 survives the decree of adoption, but failure to comply with the terms of the order or agreement is not a ground for revoking or setting aside the consent or the adoption; and

(iii) the other parent remains liable for arrearages of child support unless released from that obligation by the parent executing the consent and by a governmental entity providing public assistance to the minor.

(c) A consent may not waive further notice of the proceeding for adoption of the minor by the stepparent.

SECTION 4-106. CONTENT OF CONSENT BY MINOR'S OTHER PARENT.

(a) A consent executed by a minor's parent who is not the stepparent's spouse must be signed or confirmed in the presence of an individual specified in Section 2-405.

(b) A consent under subsection (a) must be in writing, must contain the required statements described in Section 2-406(a)(1) through (3) and (d)(3) through (6), may contain the optional statements described in Section 2-406(f), and must state that:

(1) the parent executing the consent voluntarily and unequivocally consents to the adoption of the minor by the stepparent and the transfer to the stepparent's spouse and the adoptive stepparent of any right the parent executing the consent has to legal or physical custody of the minor;

(2) the parent executing the consent understands and agrees that the adoption will terminate his or her parental relationship to the minor and will terminate any existing court order for custody, visitation, or communication with the minor, but:

(i) the minor and any descendant of the minor will retain rights of inheritance from or through the parent executing the consent;

(ii) a court order for visitation or communication with the minor by an individual related to the minor through the minor's other parent, or an agreement or order concerning another individual which is approved by the court pursuant to Section 4-113 survives the decree of adoption, but failure to comply with the terms of the order or agreement is not a ground for revoking or setting aside the consent or the adoption; and

(iii) the parent executing the consent remains liable for arrearages of child support unless released from that obligation by the other parent and any guardian ad litem of the minor and by a governmental entity providing public assistance to the minor; and

(3) the parent executing the consent has provided the adoptive stepparent with the information required by Section 2-106.

(c) A consent under subsection (a) may waive notice of the proceeding for adoption of the minor by the stepparent unless the adoption is contested, appealed, or denied.

SECTION 4-107. CONTENT OF CONSENT BY OTHER PERSONS.

(a) A consent executed by the guardian of a minor stepchild or by an agency must be in writing and signed or confirmed in the presence of the court, or in a manner the court directs, and:

(1) must state the circumstances under which the guardian or agency obtained the authority to consent to the adoption of the minor by a stepparent;

(2) must contain the statements required by Sections 4-104 and 4-105, except for any that can be made only by a parent of the minor; and

(3) may waive notice of the proceeding for adoption, unless the adoption is contested, appealed, or denied.

(b) A consent executed by a minor stepchild in a proceeding for adoption by a stepparent must be signed or confirmed in the presence of the court or in a manner the court directs.

SECTION 4-108. PETITION TO ADOPT.

(a) A petition by a stepparent to adopt a minor stepchild must be signed and verified by the petitioner and contain the following information or state why any of the information is not contained in the petition:

(1) the information required by Section 3-304(a)(1),(3),(5), and (8) through (12) and (b);

(2) the current marital status of the petitioner, including the date and place of marriage, the name and date and place of birth of the petitioner's spouse and, if the spouse is deceased, the date, place, and cause of death and, if the spouse is incompetent, the date on which a court declared the spouse incompetent;

(3) the length of time the minor has been residing with the petitioner and the petitioner's spouse and, if the minor is not in the physical custody of the petitioner and the petitioner's spouse, the reason why they do not have custody and when they intend to obtain custody; and

(4) the length of time the petitioner's spouse or the petitioner has had legal custody of the minor and the circumstances under which legal custody was obtained.

SECTION 4-109. REQUIRED DOCUMENTS.

(a) After a petition to adopt a minor stepchild is filed, the following must be filed in the proceeding:

(1) any item required by Section 3-305(a) which is relevant to an adoption by a stepparent; and

(2) a copy of any agreement to waive arrearages of child support.

(b) If any of the items required by subsection (a) is not available, the person responsible for furnishing the item shall file an affidavit explaining its absence.

SECTION 4-110. NOTICE OF PENDENCY OF PROCEEDING.

(a) Within 30 days after a petition to adopt a minor stepchild is filed, the petitioner shall serve notice of the proceeding upon:

(1) the petitioner's spouse;

(2) any other person whose consent to the adoption is required under this [article];

(3) any person described in Section 3-401(a)(3),(4), and (6) and (b); and

(4) the parents of the minor's parent whose parental relationship will be terminated by the adoption unless the identity or the whereabouts of those parents are unknown.

SECTION 4-111. EVALUATION OF STEPPARENT.

(a) After a petition for adoption of a minor stepchild is filed, the court may order that an evaluation be made by an individual qualified under Section 2-202 to assist the court in determining whether the proposed adoption is in the best interest of the minor.

(b) The court shall provide an evaluator with copies of the petition for adoption and of the items filed with the petition.

(c) Unless otherwise directed by the court, an evaluator shall base the evaluation on a personal interview with the petitioner and the petitioner's spouse in the petitioner's residence, observation of the relationship between the minor and the petitioner, personal interviews with others who know the petitioner and may have information relevant to the examination, and any information received pursuant to subsection (d).

(d) An evaluation under this section must be in writing and contain the following:

(1) the information required by Section 2-203(d) and (e);

(2) the information required by Section 3-602(b)(2) through (5); and

(3) the finding required by Section 3-602(b)(6).

(e) An evaluator shall complete an evaluation and file it with the court within 60 days after being asked for the evaluation under this section, unless the court allows a later filing.

(f) Section 3-603(b) and (c) apply to an evaluation under this section.

SECTION 4-112. DISPOSITIONAL HEARING; DECREE OF ADOPTION.

Sections 3-701 through 3-707 apply to a proceeding for adoption of a minor stepchild by a stepparent, but the court may waive the requirements of Section 3-702.

SECTION 4-113. VISITATION AGREEMENT AND ORDER.

(a) Upon the request of the petitioner in a proceeding for adoption of a minor stepchild, the court shall review a written agreement that permits another individual to visit or communicate with the minor after the decree of adoption becomes final, which must be signed by the individual, the petitioner, the petitioner's spouse, the minor if 12 years of age or older, and, if an agency placed the minor for adoption, an authorized employee of the agency.

(b) The court may enter an order approving the agreement only upon determining that the agreement is in the best interest of the minor adoptee. In making this determination, the court shall consider:

(1) the preference of the minor, if the minor is mature enough to express a preference;

(2) any special needs of the minor and how they would be affected by performance of the agreement;

(3) the length and quality of any existing relationship between the minor and the individual who would be entitled to visit or communicate, and the likely effect on the minor of allowing this relationship to continue;

(4) the specific terms of the agreement and the likelihood that the parties to the agreement will cooperate in performing its terms;

(5) the recommendation of the minor's guardian ad litem, lawyer, social worker, or other counselor; and

(6) any other factor relevant to the best interest of the minor.

(c) In addition to any agreement approved pursuant to subsections (a) and (b), the court may approve the continuation of an existing order or issue a new order permitting the minor adoptee's former parent, grandparent, or sibling to visit or communicate with the minor if:

(1) the grandparent is the parent of a deceased parent of the minor or the parent of the adoptee's parent whose parental relationship to the minor is terminated by the decree of adoption;

(2) the former parent, grandparent, or sibling requests that an existing order be permitted to survive the decree of adoption or that a new order be issued; and

(3) the court determines that the requested visitation or communication is in the best interest of the minor.

(d) In making a determination under subsection (c)(3), the court shall consider the factors listed in subsection (b) and any objections to the requested order by the adoptive stepparent and the stepparent's spouse.

(e) An order issued under this section may be enforced in a civil action only if the court finds that enforcement is in the best interest of a minor adoptee.

(f) An order issued under this section may not be modified unless the court finds that modification is in the best interest of a minor adoptee and:

(1) the individuals subject to the order request the modification; or

(2) exceptional circumstances arising since the order was issued justify the modification.

(g) Failure to comply with the terms of an order approved under this section or with any other agreement for visitation or communication is not a ground for revoking, setting aside, or otherwise challenging the validity of a consent, relinquishment, or adoption pertaining to a minor stepchild, and the validity of the consent, relinquishment, and adoption is not affected by any later action to enforce, modify, or set aside the order or agreement.

ARTICLE 5. ADOPTION OF ADULTS AND EMANCIPATED MINORS

SECTION 5-101. WHO MAY ADOPT ADULT OR EMANCIPATED MINOR.

(a) An adult may adopt another adult or an emancipated minor pursuant to this [article], but:

(1) an adult may not adopt his or her spouse; and

(2) an incompetent individual of any age may be adopted only pursuant to [Articles] 2, 3, and 4.

(b) An individual who has adopted an adult or emancipated minor may not adopt another adult or emancipated minor within one year after the adoption unless the prospective adoptee is a sibling of the adoptee.

SECTION 5-102. LEGAL CONSEQUENCES OF ADOPTION.

The legal consequences of an adoption of an adult or emancipated minor are the same as under Sections 1-103 through 1-106, but the legal consequences of adoption of an adult stepchild by an adult step-parent are the same as under Section 4-103.

SECTION 5-103. CONSENT TO ADOPTION.

(a) Consent to the adoption of an adult or emancipated minor is required only of:

(1) the adoptee;

(2) the prospective adoptive parent; and

(3) the spouse of the prospective adoptive parent, unless they are legally separated, or the court finds that the spouse is not capable of giving consent or is withholding consent contrary to the best interest of the adoptee and the prospective adoptive parent.

(b) The consent of the adoptee and the prospective adoptive parent must:

(1) be in writing and be signed or confirmed by each of them in the presence of the court or an individual authorized to take acknowledgments;

(2) state that they agree to assume toward each other the legal relationship of parent and child and to have all of the rights and be subject to all of the duties of that relationship; and

(3) state that they understand the consequences the adoption may have for any right of inheritance, property, or support each has.

(c) The consent of the spouse of the prospective adoptive parent:

(1) must be in writing and be signed or confirmed in the presence of the court or an individual authorized to take acknowledgments;

(2) must state that the spouse:

(i) consents to the proposed adoption; and

(ii) understands the consequences the adoption may have for any right of inheritance, property, or support the spouse has; and

(3) may contain a waiver of any proceeding for adoption.

SECTION 5-104. JURISDICTION AND VENUE.

(a) The court has jurisdiction over a proceeding for the adoption of an adult or emancipated minor under this [article] if a petitioner lived in this State for at least 90 days immediately preceding the filing of a petition for adoption.

(b) A petition for adoption may be filed in the court in the [county] in which a petitioner lives.

SECTION 5-105. PETITION FOR ADOPTION.

(a) A prospective adoptive parent and an adoptee under this [article] must jointly file a petition for adoption.

(b) The petition must be signed and verified by each petitioner and state:

(1) the full name, age, and place and duration of residence of each petitioner;

(2) the current marital status of each petitioner, including the date and place of marriage, if married;

(3) the full name by which the adoptee is to be known if the petition is granted;

(4) the duration and nature of the relationship between the prospective adoptive parent and the adoptee;

(5) that the prospective adoptive parent and the adoptee desire to assume the legal relationship of parent and child and to have all of the rights and be subject to all of the duties of that relationship;

(6) that the adoptee understands that a consequence of the adoption will be to terminate the adoptee's relationship as the child of an existing parent, but if the adoptive parent is the adoptee's stepparent, the adoption will not affect the adoptee's relationship with a parent who is the stepparent's spouse, but will terminate the adoptee's relationship to the adoptee's other parent, except for the right to inherit from or through that parent;

(7) the name and last known address of any other individual whose consent is required;

(8) the name, age, and last known address of any child of the prospective adoptive parent, including a child previously adopted by the prospective adoptive parent or his or her spouse, and the date and place of the adoption; and

(9) the name, age, and last known address of any living parent or child of the adoptee.

(c) The petitioners shall attach to the petition:

(1) a certified copy of the birth certificate or other evidence of the date and place of birth of the adoptee and the prospective adoptive parent, if available; and

(2) any required consent that has been executed.

SECTION 5-106. NOTICE AND TIME OF HEARING.

(a) Within 30 days after a petition for adoption is filed, the petitioners shall serve notice of hearing the petition upon any individual whose consent to the adoption is required under Section 5-103, and who has not waived notice, by sending a copy of the petition and notice of hearing to the individual at the address stated in the petition, or according to the manner of service provided in Section 3-403.

(b) The court shall set a date and time for hearing the petition, which must be at least 30 days after the notice is served.

SECTION 5-107. DISPOSITIONAL HEARING.

(a) Both petitioners shall appear in person at the hearing unless an appearance is excused for good cause shown. In the latter event an appearance may be made for either or both of them by a lawyer authorized in writing to make the appearance, or a hearing may be conducted by telephone or other electronic medium.

(b) The court shall examine the petitioners, or the lawyer for a petitioner not present in person, and shall grant the petition for adoption if it determines that:

(1) at least 30 days have elapsed since the service of notice of hearing the petition for adoption;

(2) notice has been served, or dispensed with, as to any person whose consent is required under Section 5-103;

(3) every necessary consent, waiver, document, or judicial order has been obtained and filed with the court;

(4) the adoption is for the purpose of creating the relationship of parent and child between the petitioners and the petitioners understand the consequences of the relationship; and

(5) there has been substantial compliance with this [Act].

SECTION 5-108. DECREE OF ADOPTION.

(a) A decree of adoption issued under this [article] must substantially conform to the relevant requirements of Section 3-705 and appeals from a decree, or challenges to it, are governed by Sections 3-706 and 3-707.

(b) The court shall send a copy of the decree to each individual named in the petition at the address stated in the petition.

(c) Within 30 days after a decree of adoption becomes final, the clerk of the court shall prepare a report of the adoption for the [State Registrar of Vital Records], and, if the petitioners have requested it, the report shall instruct the [Registrar] to issue a new birth certificate to the adoptee, as provided in [Article] 3, [Part] 8.

ARTICLE 6. RECORDS OF ADOPTION PROCEEDING: RETENTION, CONFIDENTIALITY, AND ACCESS

SECTION 6-101. RECORDS DEFINED.

Unless the context requires otherwise, for purposes of this [article], "records" includes all documents, exhibits, and data pertaining to an adoption.

SECTION 6-102. RECORDS CONFIDENTIAL, COURT RECORDS SEALED.

(a) All records, whether on file with the court, or in the possession of an agency, the [Registrar of Vital Records or Statistics], a lawyer, or another provider of professional services in connection with an adoption, are confidential and may not be inspected except as provided in this [Act].

(b) During a proceeding for adoption, records are not open to inspection except as directed by the court.

(c) Within 30 days after a decree of adoption becomes final, the clerk of the court shall send to the [Registrar], in addition to the report of adoption required by Section 3-801, a certified copy of any document signed pursuant to Section 2-404(e) and filed in the proceeding for adoption.

(d) All records on file with the court must be retained permanently and sealed for 99 years after the date of the adoptee's birth. Sealed records and indices of the records are not open to inspection by any person except as provided in this [Act].

(e) Any additional information about an adoptee, the adoptee's former parents, and the adoptee's genetic history that is submitted to the court within the 99-year period, must be added to the sealed records of the court. Any additional information that is submitted to an agency, lawyer, or other professional provider of services within the 99-year period must be kept confidential.

SECTION 6-103. RELEASE OF NONIDENTIFYING INFORMATION.

(a) An adoptive parent or guardian of an adoptee, an adoptee who has attained 18 years of age, an emancipated adoptee, a deceased adoptee's direct descendant who has attained 18 years of age, or the parent or guardian of a direct descendant who has not attained 18 years of age may request the court that granted the adoption or the agency that placed the adoptee for adoption, to furnish the nonidentifying information about the adoptee, the adoptee's former parents, and the adoptee's genetic history that has been retained by the court or agency, including the information required by Section 2-106.

(b) The court or agency shall furnish the individual who makes the request with a detailed summary of any relevant report or information that is included in the sealed records of the court or the confidential records of the agency. The summary must exclude identifying information concerning an individual who has not filed a waiver of confidentiality with the court or agency. The department or the court shall prescribe forms and a procedure for summarizing any report or information released under this section.

(c) An individual who is denied access to nonidentifying information to which the individual is entitled under this [article] or Section 2-106 may petition the court for relief.

(d) If a court receives a certified statement from a physician which explains in detail how a health condition may seriously affect the health of the adoptee or a direct descendant of the adoptee, the court shall make a diligent effort to notify an adoptee who has attained 18 years of age, an adoptive parent or guardian of an adoptee who has not attained 18 years of age, or a direct descendant of a deceased adoptee that the nonidentifying information is available and may be requested from the court.

(e) If a court receives a certified statement from a physician which explains in detail why a serious health condition of the adoptee or a direct descendant of the adoptee should be communicated to the adoptee's genetic parent or sibling to enable them to make an informed reproductive decision, the court shall make a diligent effort to notify those individuals that the nonidentifying information is available and may be requested from the court.

(f) If the [Registrar] receives a request or any additional information from an individual pursuant to this section, the [Registrar] shall give the individual the name and address of the court or agency having the records, and if the court or agency is in another State, shall assist the individual in locating the court or agency. The [Registrar] shall prescribe a reasonable procedure for verifying the identity, age, or other relevant characteristics of an individual who requests or furnishes information under this section.

SECTION 6-104. DISCLOSURE OF IDENTIFYING INFORMATION.

(a) Except as otherwise provided in this [article], identifying information about an adoptee's former parent, an adoptee, or an adoptive parent which is contained in records, including original birth certificates, required by this [Act] to be confidential or sealed, may not be disclosed to any person.

(b) Identifying information about an adoptee's former parent must be disclosed by the [Registrar] to an adoptee who has attained 18 years of age, an adoptive parent or guardian of an adoptee who has not attained 18 years of age, a deceased adoptee's direct descendant who has attained 18 years of age, or the parent or guardian of a direct descendant who has not attained 18 years of age if one of these individuals requests the information and:

(1) the adoptee's former parent or, if the former parent is deceased or has been judicially declared incompetent, an adult descendant of the former parent authorizes the disclosure of his or her name, date of birth, or last known address, or other identifying information, either in a document signed pursuant to Section 2-404(e) and filed in the proceeding for adoption or in another signed document filed with the court, an agency, or the [Registrar]; or

(2) the adoptee's former parent authorizes the disclosure of the requested information only if the adoptee, adoptive parent, or direct descendant agrees to release similar identifying information about the adoptee, adoptive parent, or direct descendant and this individual authorizes the disclosure of the information in a signed document kept by the court, an agency, or the [Registrar].

(c) Identifying information about an adoptee or a deceased adoptee's direct descendant must be disclosed by the [Registrar] to an adoptee's former parent if that individual requests the information and:

(1) an adoptee who has attained 18 years of age, an adoptive parent or guardian of an adoptee who has not attained 18 years of age, a deceased adoptee's direct descendant who has attained 18 years of age, or the parent or guardian of a direct descendant

who has not attained 18 years of age authorizes the disclosure of the requested information in a signed document kept by the court, an agency, or the [Registrar]; or

(2) one of the individuals listed in paragraph (1) authorizes the disclosure of the requested information only if the adoptee's former parent agrees to release similar information about himself or herself, and the former parent authorizes the disclosure of the information in a signed document kept by the court, an agency, or the [Registrar].

(d) Identifying information about an adult sibling of an adoptee who has attained 18 years of age must be disclosed by the [Registrar] to an adoptee if the sibling is also an adoptee and both the sibling and the adoptee authorize the disclosure.

(e) Subsection (d) does not permit disclosure of a former parent's identity unless that parent has authorized disclosure under this [Act].

SECTION 6-105. ACTION FOR DISCLOSURE OF INFORMATION.

(a) To obtain information not otherwise available under Section 6-103 or 6-104, an adoptee who has attained 18 years of age, an adoptee who has not attained 18 years of age and has the permission of an adoptive parent or guardian, an adoptive parent or guardian of an adoptee who has not attained 18 years of age, a deceased adoptee's direct descendant who has attained 18 years of age, the parent or guardian of a direct descendant who has not attained 18 years of age, or an adoptee's former parent may file a petition in the court to obtain information about another individual described in this section which is contained in records, including original birth certificates, required by this [Act] to be confidential or sealed.

(b) In determining whether to grant a petition under this section, the court shall review the sealed records of the relevant proceeding for adoption and shall make specific findings concerning:

(1) the reason the information is sought;

(2) whether the individual about whom information is sought has filed a signed document described in Section 2-404(e) or 6-104 requesting that his or her identity not be disclosed, or has not filed any document;

(3) whether the individual about whom information is sought is alive;

(4) whether it is possible to satisfy the petitioner's request without disclosing the identity of another individual;

(5) the likely effect of disclosure on the adoptee, the adoptive parents, the adoptee's former parents, and other members of the adoptee's original and adoptive families; and

(6) the age, maturity, and expressed needs of the adoptee.

(c) The court may order the disclosure of the requested information only upon a determination that good cause exists for the release based on the findings required by subsection (b) and a conclusion that:

(1) there is a compelling reason for disclosure of the information; and

(2) the benefit to the petitioner will be greater than the harm to any other individual of disclosing the information.

SECTION 6-106. STATEWIDE REGISTRY.

The [Registrar] shall:

(1) establish a statewide confidential registry for receiving, filing, and retaining documents requesting, authorizing, or not authorizing, the release of identifying information;

(2) prescribe and distribute forms or documents on which an individual may request, authorize, or refuse to authorize the release of identifying information;

(3) devise a procedure for releasing identifying information in the [Registrar's] possession upon receipt of an appropriate request and authorization;

(4) cooperate with registries in other States to facilitate the matching of documents filed pursuant to this [article] by individuals in different States; and

(5) announce and publicize to the general public the existence of the registry and the procedure for the consensual release of identifying information.

SECTION 6-107. RELEASE OF ORIGINAL BIRTH CERTIFICATE.

(a) In addition to any copy of an adoptee's original birth certificate authorized for release by a court order issued pursuant to Section 6-105, the [Registrar] shall furnish a copy of the original birth certificate upon the request of an adoptee who has attained 18 years of age, the direct descendant of a deceased adoptee, or an adoptive parent or guardian of an adoptee who has not attained 18 years of age, if the individual who makes the request furnishes a consent to disclosure signed by each individual who was named as a parent on the adoptee's original birth certificate.

(b) When 99 years have elapsed after the date of birth of an adoptee whose original birth certificate is sealed under this [Act], the [Registrar] shall unseal the original certificate and file it with any new or amended certificate that has been issued. The unsealed certificates become public information in accordance with any statute or regulation applicable to the retention and disclosure of records by the [Registrar].

SECTION 6-108. CERTIFICATE OF ADOPTION.

Upon the request of an adoptive parent or an adoptee who has attained 18 years of age, the clerk of the court that entered a decree of adoption shall issue a certificate of adoption which states the date and place of adoption, the date of birth of the adoptee, the name of each adoptive parent, and the name of the adoptee as provided in the decree.

SECTION 6-109. DISCLOSURE AUTHORIZED IN COURSE OF EMPLOYMENT.

This [article] does not preclude an employee or agent of a court, agency, or the [Registrar] from:

(1) inspecting permanent, confidential, or sealed records for the purpose of discharging any obligation under this [Act];

(2) disclosing the name of the court where a proceeding for adoption occurred, or the name of an agency that placed an adoptee, to an individual described in Sections 6-103 through 6-105, who can verify his or her identity; or

(3) disclosing nonidentifying information contained in confidential or sealed records in accordance with any other applicable state or federal law.

SECTION 6-110. FEE FOR SERVICES.

A court, an agency, or the [Registrar] may charge a reasonable fee for services, including copying services, it performs pursuant to this [article].

ARTICLE 7. PROHIBITED AND PERMISSIBLE ACTIVITIES IN CONNECTION WITH ADOPTION

SECTION 7-101. PROHIBITED ACTIVITIES IN PLACEMENT.

(a) Except as otherwise provided in [Article] 2, [Part] 1:
(1) a person, other than a parent, guardian, or agency, as specified in Sections 2-101 through 2-103, may not place a minor for adoption or advertise in any public medium that the person knows of a minor who is available for adoption;

(2) a person, other than an agency or an individual with a favorable preplacement evaluation, as required by Sections 2-201 through 2-207, may not advertise in any public medium that the person is willing to accept a minor for adoption;

(3) an individual, other than a relative or stepparent of a minor, who does not have a favorable preplacement evaluation or a court-ordered waiver of the evaluation, or who has an unfavorable evaluation, may not obtain legal or physical custody of a minor for purposes of adoption; and

(4) a person may not place or assist in placing a minor for adoption with an individual, other than a relative or stepparent, unless the person knows that the individual has a favorable preplacement evaluation or a waiver pursuant to Section 2-201.

(b) A person who violates subsection (a) is liable for a [civil penalty] not to exceed [$5,000] for the first violation, and not to exceed [$10,000] for each succeeding violation in an action brought by the [appropriate official]. The court may enjoin from further violations any person who violates subsection (a) and shall inform any appropriate licensing authority or other official of the violation.

SECTION 7-102. UNLAWFUL PAYMENTS RELATED TO ADOPTION.

(a) Except as otherwise provided in Sections 7-103 and 7-104, a person may not pay or give or offer to pay or give to any other person, or request, receive, or accept any money or anything of value, directly or indirectly, for:

(1) the placement of a minor for adoption;

(2) the consent of a parent, a guardian, or an agency to the adoption of a minor; or

(3) the relinquishment of a minor to an agency for the purpose of adoption.

(b) The following persons are liable for a [civil penalty] not to exceed [$5,000] for the first violation, and not to exceed [$10,000] for each succeeding violation in an action brought by the [appropriate official]:

(1) a person who knowingly violates subsection (a);

(2) a person who knowingly makes a false report to the court about a payment prohibited by this section or authorized by Section 7-103 or 7-104; and

(3) a parent or guardian who knowingly receives or accepts a payment authorized by Section 7-103 or 7-104 with the intent not to consent to an adoption or to relinquish a minor for adoption.

(c) The court may enjoin from further violations any person described in subsection (b) and shall inform any appropriate licensing authority or other official of the violation.

SECTION 7-103. LAWFUL PAYMENTS RELATED TO ADOPTION.

(a) Subject to the requirements of Sections 3-702 and 3-703 for an accounting and judicial approval of fees and charges related to an adoption, an adoptive parent, or a person acting on behalf of an adoptive parent, may pay for:

(1) the services of an agency in connection with an adoption;

(2) advertising and similar expenses incurred in locating a minor for adoption;

(3) medical, hospital, nursing, pharmaceutical, travel, or other similar expenses incurred by a mother or her minor child in connection with the birth or any illness of the minor;

(4) counseling services for a parent or a minor for a reasonable time before and after the minor's placement for adoption;

(5) living expenses of a mother for a reasonable time before the birth of her child and for no more than six weeks after the birth;

(6) expenses incurred in ascertaining the information required by Section 2-106;

(7) legal services, court costs, and travel or other administrative expenses connected with an adoption, including any legal services performed for a parent who consents to the adoption of a minor or relinquishes the minor to an agency;

(8) expenses incurred in obtaining a preplacement evaluation and an evaluation during the proceeding for adoption; and

(9) any other service the court finds is reasonably necessary.

(b) A parent or a guardian, a person acting on the parent's or guardian's behalf, or a provider of a service listed in subsection (a), may receive or accept a payment authorized by subsection (a). The payment may not be made contingent on the placement of a minor for adoption, relinquishment of the minor, or consent to the adoption. If the adoption is not completed, a person who is authorized to make a specific payment by subsection (a) is not liable for that payment unless the person has agreed in a signed writing with a provider of a service to make the payment regardless of the outcome of the proceeding for adoption.

SECTION 7-104. CHARGES BY AGENCY.

Subject to the requirements of Sections 3-702 and 3-703 for an accounting and judicial approval of fees and charges related to an adoption, an agency may charge or accept a fee or other reasonable compensation from a prospective adoptive parent for:

(1) medical, hospital, nursing, pharmaceutical, travel, or other similar expenses incurred by a mother or her minor child in connection with the birth or any illness of the minor;

(2) a percentage of the annual cost the agency incurs in locating and providing counseling services for minor adoptees, parents, and prospective parents;

(3) living expenses of a mother for a reasonable time before the birth of a child and for no more than six weeks after the birth;

(4) expenses incurred in ascertaining the information required by Section 2-106;

(5) legal services, court costs, and travel or other administrative expenses connected with an adoption, including the legal services performed for a parent who relinquishes a minor child to the agency;

(6) preparation of a preplacement evaluation and an evaluation during the proceeding for adoption; and

(7) any other service the court finds is reasonably necessary.

SECTION 7-105. FAILURE TO DISCLOSE INFORMATION.

(a) A person, other than a parent, who has a duty to furnish the nonidentifying information required by Section 2-106, or authorized for release under [Article] 6, and who intentionally refuses to provide the information is subject to a [civil penalty] not to exceed [$5,000] for the first violation, and not to exceed [$10,000] for each succeeding violation in an action brought by the [appropriate official]. The court may enjoin the person from further violations of the duty to furnish nonidentifying information.

(b) An employee or agent of an agency, the court, or the [State Registrar of Vital Records] who intentionally destroys any information or report compiled pursuant to Section 2-106, or authorized for release under [Article] 6, is guilty of a [misdemeanor] [punishable upon conviction by a fine of not more than [$] or imprisonment for not more than [   ], or both].

(c) In addition to the penalties provided in subsections (a) and (b), an adoptive parent, an adoptee, or any person who is the subject of any information required by Section 2-106, or authorized for release under [Article] 6, may maintain an action for damages or equitable relief against a person, other than a parent who placed a minor for adoption, who fails to perform the duties required by Section 2-106 or [Article] 6.

(d) A prospective adoptive parent who knowingly fails to furnish information or knowingly furnishes false information to an evaluator preparing an evaluation pursuant to [Article] 2, [Part] 2 or [Article] 3, [Part] 6, with the intent to deceive the evaluator, is guilty of a [misdemeanor] [punishable upon conviction by a fine of not more than [$] or imprisonment for not more than [   ], or both].

(e) An evaluator who prepares an evaluation pursuant to [Article] 2, [Part] 2 or [Article] 3, [Part] 6 and who knowingly omits or misrepresents information about the individual being evaluated with the intent to deceive a person authorized under this [Act] to place a minor for adoption is guilty of a [misdemeanor] [punishable upon conviction by a fine of not more than [$] or imprisonment for not more than [   ], or both].

(f) A parent of a minor child who knowingly misidentifies the minor's other parent with an intent to deceive the other parent, an agency, or a prospective adoptive parent is subject to a [civil penalty] not to exceed [$5,000] in an action brought by the [appropriate official].

SECTION 7-106. UNAUTHORIZED DISCLOSURE OF INFORMATION.

(a) Except as authorized in this [Act], a person who furnishes or retains a report or records pursuant to this [Act] may not disclose any identifying or nonidentifying information contained in the report or records.

(b) A person who knowingly gives or offers to give or who accepts or agrees to accept anything of value for an unauthorized disclosure of identifying information made confidential by this [Act] is guilty of a [misdemeanor] [punishable upon conviction by a fine of not more than [$] or imprisonment for not more than [   ], or both,] for the first violation and of a [felony] [punishable upon conviction by a fine of not more than [$] or imprisonment for not more than [   ], or both,] for each succeeding violation.

(c) A person who knowingly gives or offers to give or who accepts or agrees to accept anything of value for an unauthorized disclosure of nonidentifying information made confidential by this [Act] is subject to a [civil penalty] not to exceed [$5,000] for the first violation, and not to exceed [$10,000] for each succeeding violation in an action brought by the [appropriate official].

(d) A person who makes a disclosure, that the person knows is unauthorized, of identifying or nonidentifying information from a report or record made confidential by this [Act] is subject to a [civil penalty] not to exceed [$2,500] for the first violation, and not to exceed [$5,000] for each succeeding violation in an action brought by the [appropriate official].

(e) The court may enjoin from further violations any person who makes or obtains an unauthorized disclosure and shall inform any appropriate licensing authority or other official of the violation.

(f) In addition to the penalties provided in subsections (b) through (e), an individual who is the subject of any of the information contained in a report or records made confidential by this [Act] may maintain an action for damages or equitable relief against any person who makes or obtains, or is likely to make or obtain, an unauthorized disclosure of the information.

(g) Identifying information contained in a report or records required by this [Act] to be kept confidential or sealed may not be disclosed under any other law of this State.

SECTION 7-107. ACTION BY DEPARTMENT.

The department may review and investigate compliance with this [Act] and may maintain an action in the [appropriate court] to compel compliance.

ARTICLE 8. MISCELLANEOUS PROVISIONS

SECTION 8-101. UNIFORMITY OF APPLICATION AND CONSTRUCTION.

This [Act] shall be applied and construed to effectuate its general purpose to make uniform the law with respect to the subject of this [Act] among the States enacting it.

SECTION 8-102. SHORT TITLE.

This [Act] may be cited as the Uniform Adoption Act(1994).

SECTION 8-103. SEVERABILITY CLAUSE.

If any provision of this [Act] or its application to any person or circumstance is held invalid, the invalidity does not affect other provisions or application of this [Act] which can be given effect without the invalid provision or application, and to this end the provisions of this [Act] are severable.

SECTION 8-104. EFFECTIVE DATE.

This [Act] takes effect on ....

SECTION 8-105. REPEALS.

The following acts and parts of acts are repealed:

(1) ....

(2) ....

(3) ....

SECTION 8-106. TRANSITIONAL PROVISIONS.

A proceeding for adoption commenced before the effective date of this [Act] may be completed under the law in effect at the time the proceeding was commenced.

Source: National Conference of Commissioners on Uniform State Laws

APPENDIX 4:
TABLE OF STATE STATUTES GOVERNING ADVERTISING IN PRIVATE PLACEMENT ADOPTIONS

STATE	STATUTE
Alabama	Alabama Code § 26-10A-36
Alaska	Not Addressed in Statute
Arizona	Not Addressed in Statute
Arkansas	Not Addressed in Statute
California	California Family Law § 8609(a)
Colorado	Not Addressed in Statute
Connecticut	Connecticut Gen. Statutes §§ 45a-728(d)
Delaware	Delaware Ann. Code Tit. 13 § 930
District of Columbia	Not Addressed in Statute
Florida	Florida Ann. Statutes §§ 63.212(1)(g)
Georgia	Georgia Ann. Code § 19-8-24(a)
Hawaii	Not Addressed in Statute
Idaho	Idaho Ann. Code § 18-1512A(1)
Illinois	Not Addressed in Statute
Indiana	Not Addressed in Statute
Iowa	Not Addressed in Statute
Kansas	Kansas Ann. Statutes § 59-2123(a)(1), (b)-(c)

STATE	STATUTE
Kentucky	Kentucky Revised Statutes § 199.590(1)
Louisiana	Louisiana Rev. Stat. § 46:1425(A)
Maine	Maine Revised Statutes Tit. 18-A, § 9-313
Maryland	Not Addressed in Statute
Massachusetts	Massachusetts Ann. Laws. Ch. 28A, § 14
Michigan	Not Addressed in Statute
Minnesota	Not Addressed in Statute
Mississippi	Not Addressed in Statute
Missouri	Not Addressed in Statute
Montana	Montana Ann. Code § 42-7-105(1)(a)
Nebraska	Nebraska Revised Statutes § 43-701
Nevada	Nevada Revised Statutes §§ 127.283; 127.310(1)
New Hampshire	New Hampshire Revised Statutes § 170-E:39
New Jersey	Not Addressed in Statute
New Mexico	Not Addressed in Statute
New York	Not Addressed in Statute
North Carolina	North Carolina General Statutes § 48-10-101(b)-(b1)
North Dakota	North Dakota Cent. Code §§ 23-16-08; 50-11-06; 50-19-11
Ohio	Ohio Revised Code § 5103.17
Oklahoma	Oklahoma Ann. Statutes Tit. 21, § 866(A)(1)(g)-(h)
Oregon	Oregon Revised Statutes § 109.311(4)
Pennsylvania	Not Addressed in Statute
Rhode Island	Not Addressed in Statute
South Carolina	Not Addressed in Statute
South Dakota	Not Addressed in Statute
Tennessee	Not Addressed in Statute
Texas	Texas Penal Code § 25.09
Utah	Utah Ann. Code § 62A-4a-602(2)(b)
Vermont	Not Addressed in Statute

STATE	STATUTE
Virginia	Virginia Ann. Code §§ 63.2-1218; 63.2-1225
Washington	Washington Rev. Code § 26.33.400(1)-(2)
West Virginia	Not Addressed in Statute
Wisconsin	Wisconsin Ann. Statutes § 48.825
Wyoming	Not Addressed in Statute

Source: Child Welfare Information Gateway

APPENDIX 5:
TABLE OF STATE STATUTES GOVERNING THE USE OF INTERMEDIARIES IN PRIVATE PLACEMENT ADOPTIONS

STATE	STATUTE
Alabama	Alabama Code § 26-10A-34
Alaska	Not Addressed in Statute
Arizona	Not Addressed in Statute
Arkansas	Not Addressed in Statute
California	California Family Law §§ 8623 - 8638
Colorado	Colorado Rev. Stat. § 19-5-213
Connecticut	Not Addressed in Statute
Delaware	Delaware Ann. Code Tit. 13 §§ 904p 906
District of Columbia	D.C. Ann. Code § 4-1405(a)
Florida	Florida Ann. Statutes §§ 63.032; 63.039; 63.085
Georgia	Georgia Ann. Code § 19-8-24(a)(2)
Hawaii	Not Addressed in Statute
Idaho	Not Addressed in Statute
Illinois	Not Addressed in Statute
Indiana	Not Addressed in Statute
Iowa	Not Addressed in Statute
Kansas	Kansas Ann. Statutes § 59-2123(a)(2)-(3)

STATE	STATUTE
Kentucky	Kentucky Revised Statutes § 199.590(3), (5)
Louisiana	Louisiana Rev. Stat. § 46:1425(B)-(C)
Maine	Not Addressed in Statute
Maryland	Maryland Fam. Law § 5-38-32
Massachusetts	Massachusetts Ann. Law Ch. 28A, § 11(c)
Michigan	Michigan Comp. Laws §§ 722.123b©-(d); 722.956
Minnesota	Minnesota Ann. Stat. §§ 259.21; 259.47
Mississippi	Not Addressed in Statute
Missouri	Missouri Ann. Stat. § 568.175
Montana	Montana Ann. Code § 42-7-105(1)(b); 52-8-101
Nebraska	Nebraska Revised Statutes § 43-701
Nevada	Nevada Revised Statutes §§ 127.240; 127.285(1)
New Hampshire	Not Addressed in Statute
New Jersey	New Jersey Ann. Stat. §§ 9:3-38(1); 9:3-39.1(a)(4)
New Mexico	New Mexico Ann. Stat. § 32A-5.42(A)
New York	New York Social Services Law § 374(2)
North Carolina	North Carolina Gen. Stat. §§ 48-1-101(3a); 48-3-201; 48-3-202; 48-10-101
North Dakota	Not Addressed in Statute
Ohio	Ohio Revised Code § 3107.011(A)
Oklahoma	Oklahoma Ann. Statutes Tit. 21, § 866(A)(1)(a)-(c)
Oregon	Oregon Revised Statutes § 109.311(3)
Pennsylvania	Pennsylvania Cons. Stat. Tit. 23, §§ 2102; 2530; 2533
Rhode Island	Not Addressed in Statute
South Carolina	South Carolina Ann. Laws §§ 20-7-1650(a); 20-7-1690(F); 20-7-1730(A)(11)
South Dakota	South Dakota Ann. Stat. § 25-6-4.2
Tennessee	Tennessee Ann. Code § 36-1-108(a)
Texas	Texas Penal Code § 25.08(a)-(b)

STATE	STATUTE
Utah	Utah Ann. Code § 62A-4a-602(1), (2)(a), (3)
Vermont	Vermont Ann. Stat. Tit. 15A,, § 2-102(a)-(d)
Virginia	Virginia Ann. Code § 63.2-1218
Washington	Washington Rev. Code § 26.33.390(2)-(3)
West Virginia	West Virginia Ann. Code § 48-22-803
Wisconsin	Not Addressed in Statute
Wyoming	Not Addressed in Statute

Source: Child Welfare Information Gateway

APPENDIX 6:
TABLE OF STATE STATUTES GOVERNING COURT JURISDICTION AND VENUE OVER ADOPTION PROCEEDINGS

STATE	JURISDICTION	VENUE
Alabama	Alabama Code § 26-10A-3	Alabama Code § 26-10A-4
Alaska	Alaska Stat. § 25.23.030	Alaska Stat. § 25.23.030
Arizona	Arizona Rev. Stat. § 8-102.01	Arizona Rev. Stat. § 8-104
Arkansas	Arkansas Ann. Code §§ 9-9-202(2); 205(3)(B); 9-27-306(a)	Arkansas Ann. Code §§ 9-9-205(c); 9-27-307
California	California Fam. Code § 200; Welf. & Inst. Code § 366.3	California Fam. Code §§ 8714; 8802; 9000; Welf. & Inst. Code § 366.3
Colorado	Colorado Rev. Stat. § 19-1-104(1)	Colorado Rev. Stat. § 19-5-204
Connecticut	Connecticut Ann. Stat. 45a-717	Connecticut Ann. Stat. 45a-717(a)(4)
Delaware	Delaware Ann. Code Tit. 13, § 902	Delaware Ann. Code Tit. 13, § 902(b)
District of Columbia	District of Columbia Ann. Code § 16-301	Not Addressed in Statute
Florida	Florida Ann. Stat. § 63.102(1)	Florida Ann. Stat. § 63.102(2)
Georgia	Georgia Ann. Code § 19-8-2(a)	Georgia Ann. Code § 19-8-2(b)

STATE	JURISDICTION	VENUE
Hawaii	Hawaii Rev. Stat. § 578-1	Hawaii Rev. Stat. § 578-1
Idaho	Idaho Ann. Code § 16-1506	Idaho Ann. Code § 16-1506
Illinois	Illinois Comp. Stat. Ch. 750 § 50/4	Illinois Comp. Stat. Ch. 750 § 50/4
Indiana	Indiana Ann. Stat. §§ 31-19-1-2; 2-1	Indiana Ann. Stat. §§ 31-19-2-2; 2-3
Iowa	Iowa Ann. Stat. § 600.30	Iowa Ann. Stat. § 600.3
Kansas	Kansas Ann. Stat. § 59-2127	Kansas Ann. Stat. § 59-2126
Kentucky	Kentucky Ann. Stat. § 199.470	Kentucky Ann. Stat. § 199.470
Louisiana	Louisiana Children's Code Art. 1180	Louisiana Children's Code Art. 1180
Maine	Maine Rev. Stat. Tit. 18-A, § 9-103	Maine Rev. Stat. Tit. 18-A, § 9-104
Maryland	Maryland Fam. Law § 1-201	Cts. & Jud. Pro. § 6-203(e)
Massachusetts	Massachusetts Ann. Laws Ch. 210, § 1	Massachusetts Ann. Laws Ch. 210, § 1
Michigan	Michigan Comp. Laws § 710.22	Michigan Comp. Laws § 710.24
Minnesota	Minnesota Ann. Stat. § 259.23, subd. 1	Minnesota Ann. Stat. § 259.23, subd. 1
Mississippi	Mississippi Ann. Code § 93-17-3	Mississippi Ann. Code § 93-17-3
Missouri	Missouri Ann. Stat. § 453.010	Missouri Ann. Stat. § 453.010
Montana	Montana Ann. Code § 42-1-104	Montana Ann. Code § 42-1-104
Nebraska	Nebraska Rev. Stat. § 43-102	Nebraska Rev. Stat. § 43-102
Nevada	Nevada Rev. Stat. § 127.010	Nevada Rev. Stat. § 127.030
New Hampshire	New Hampshire Rev. Stat. § 170-B:15	New Hampshire Rev. Stat. § 170-B:15

STATE	JURISDICTION	VENUE
New Jersey	New Jersey Ann. Stat. § 9:3-42	New Jersey Ann. Stat. § 9:3-42
New Mexico	New Mexico Ann. Stat. §§ 32A-1-4; 32A-1-9	New Mexico Ann. Stat. § 32A-5-10
New York	New York Fam. Ct. §§ 115, 641	New York Dom. Rel. §§ 113(3); 115
North Carolina	North Carolina Gen. Stat. § 48-2-100	North Carolina Gen. Stat. § 48-2-101
North Dakota	North Dakota Cent. Code § 14-15-01	North Dakota Cent. Code § 14-15-04
Ohio	Ohio Rev. Code § 3107.01	Ohio Rev. Code § 3107.04
Oklahoma	Oklahoma Rev. Stat. tit. 10, § 7502-1.1	Oklahoma Rev. Stat. tit. 10, § 7502-1.2
Oregon	Oregon Rev. Stat. § 109.309(1)-(3)	Oregon Rev. Stat. § 109.309(5)
Pennsylvania	Pennsylvania Cons. Stat. Tit. 23, § 2301	Pennsylvania Cons. Stat. Tit. 23, §2302
Rhode Island	Rhode Island Gen. Laws § 15-7-4	Rhode Island Gen. Laws § 15-7-4
South Carolina	South Carolina Ann. Code § 20-7-1680	South Carolina Ann. Code § 20-7-1680
South Dakota	South Dakota Ann. Stat. § 25-6-6	South Dakota Ann. Stat. § 25-6-7
Tennessee	Tennessee Ann. Code § 36-1-102(16)	Tennessee Ann. Code § 36-1-114
Texas	Texas Fam. Code § 101.008	Texas Fam. Code § 103.001(b)
Utah	Utah Ann. Code §§ 78-30-7; 78-3a-104(1)(p)	Utah Ann. Code § 78-30-7
Vermont	Vermont Ann. Stat. Tit. 15A, § 3-101	Vermont Ann. Stat. Tit. 15A, § 3-102
Virginia	Virginia Ann. Code § 63.2-1201	Virginia Ann. Code § 63.2-1201
Washington	Washington Rev. Code § 26.33.030	Washington Rev. Code § 26.33.030

STATE	JURISDICTION	VENUE
West Virginia	West Virginia Ann. Code § 48-22-201	West Virginia Ann. Code § 48-22-201
Wisconsin	Wisconsin Ann. Stat. § 48.83	Wisconsin Ann. Stat. § 48.83
Wyoming	Wyoming Ann. Stat. § 1-22-104	Wyoming Ann. Stat. § 1-5-108

Source: Child Welfare Information Gateway

APPENDIX 7:
TABLE OF STATE STATUTES GOVERNING CRIMINAL BACKGROUND CHECKS FOR PROSPECTIVE ADOPTIVE PARENTS

STATE	STATUTE
Alabama	Alabama Code §§ 26-10A-19; 38-13-3(5); Ala. Admin. Code r. 660-5-22-03
Alaska	Alaska Admin. Code tit. 7, §§ 56.660; 56.210(b)
Arizona	Arizona Rev. Stat. §§ 8-105(D) & (E); 8-112(B)(6) & (7)
Arkansas	Arkansas Ann. Code §§ 9-9-212(b)(5)-(8); 016 15 Code of Ark. Rules & Regs. 011
California	California Family Law §§ 8712; 8730; 8811; 8908
Colorado	Colorado Rev. Stat. §§ 19-5-207 (2.5)(a); 19-5-208(5)
Connecticut	Connecticut Gen. Stat. § 17a-114(b)(2)
Delaware	Delaware Ann. Code Tit. 31, § 309; Code of Del. Regs. § 9-300-301, Rule 26 & 27
District of Columbia	D.C. Ann. Code §§ 4-1305.02; 4-1305.06; Code of D.C. Regs. § 29-1620(5)(q)
Florida	Florida Ann. Statutes §§ 63.002; 63.089(4)(b)(2); Admin. Code § 65C-16.007
Georgia	Georgia Ann. Code § 19-8-16; Rules & Regs. § 290-9-2-.06
Hawaii	Hawaii Rev. Stat. § 346-19.7(b), (d)
Idaho	Idaho Code § 16-1506(3); Admin. Code § 16.05.06.015
Illinois	Ill. Comp. Stat. § 50/6; 89 Ill. Admin. Code § 402.28

STATE	STATUTE
Indiana	Indiana Ann. Code §§ 31-19-2-7.5; 31-9-2-22.5; 31-19-8-6
Iowa	Iowa Ann. Code § 600.8; Admin. Code § 441.107.8
Kansas	Kansas Ann. Statutes § 59-2132
Kentucky	Kentucky Rev. Stat. § 199.462; 922 Ky. Admin. Reg. 1:490
Louisiana	Louisiana Children's Code art. 1131; Rev. Stat. §§ 46.282; 46.51.2
Maine	Maine Rev. Stat. Ann. Tit. 18-A, § 9-304
Maryland	Maryland Fam. Law §§ 5-561; 5-562; Code of Md. Regs. §§ 07.02.12.10; 07.05.03.09
Massachusetts	Massachusetts Gen. Laws ch. 210, § 3B; 110 Code of Mass. Reg. §§ 18.08; 18.10
Michigan	Michigan Comp. Laws Ann. § 710.23f
Minnesota	Minnesota Ann. Stat. § 259.41, Subd. 3
Mississippi	Mississippi Ann. Code § 93-17-11; Code of Miss. Rules § 11-111-001
Missouri	Missouri Rev. Stat. § 453.070(3); 13 Mo. Code of State Reg. § 40-59.030
Montana	Montana Ann. Code § 42-3-203
Nebraska	Nebraska Rev. Stat. § 43-107
Nevada	Nevada Rev. Stat. § 127.281; Admin. Code §§ 127.235; 127.240
New Hampshire	New Hampshire Rev. Stat. Ann. § 170-B:18(VI); Admin. Rules § He-C 6448.13
New Jersey	New Jersey Ann. Stat. §§ 9:3-54.2; 30:4C-26.8; Admin. Code § 10:121A-5.6
New Mexico	New Mexico Ann. Stat. §§ 32A-5-14; 32A-5-14.1; Admin. Code §§ 8.26.3.18; 8.26.2.11
New York	New York Dom. Rel. Law §§ 112; 115-d
North Carolina	North Carolina Gen. Stat. § 48-3-309; Admin. Code Tit. 10A, § 70H.0108
North Dakota	North Dakota Cent. Code § 14-15-11
Ohio	Ohio Rev. Code Ann. § 2151.86

STATE	STATUTE
Oklahoma	Oklahoma Ann. Stat. Tit. 10, § 7505-5.3(A); Admin. Code §§ 340:75-15-87; 340:75-15-88
Oregon	Not Addressed in Statute
Pennsylvania	Pennsylvania Cons. Stat. Tit. 23, § 6344
Rhode Island	Rhode Island Gen. Laws § 15-7-11; Code of R.I. Rules 03-240-806
South Carolina	South Carolina Ann. Code § 20-7-1740(A)(1)(c)
South Dakota	South Dakota Codified Laws § 25-6-9.1
Tennessee	Tennessee Ann. Code § 36-1-116; Code of Rules & Regs. R. 0250-4-9-.09
Texas	Texas Fam. Code § 162.0085; Govt. Code § 411.114; Admin. Code Tit. 40; § 745.651-655
Utah	Utah Ann. Code §§ 78-30-3.5; 78-30-3.6; Admin. Code R501-14-1; R501-14-4
Vermont	Vermont Ann. Stat. Tit. 15A § 1-113
Virginia	Virginia Ann. Code § 63.2-1721
Washington	Washington Rev. Code § 26.33.190; Admin. Code §§ 388-06-0110, 0150, 0170, 0180
West Virginia	West Virginia Ann. Code § 48-22-701; Code of State Rules § 78-2-13
Wisconsin	Wisconsin Ann. Stat. § 48.88; Admin. Code HFS 12.09; HFS 51.07
Wyoming	Wyoming Ann. Stat. § 1-22-104; Code of Wy. Rules § 049-040-001

Source: Child Welfare Information Gateway

APPENDIX 8:
TABLE OF ALLOWABLE
ADOPTION EXPENSES

STATE	BIRTH PARENT EXPENSES	PAYMENT FOR ARRANGING ADOPTION	PAYMENT FOR RELINQUISHING CHILD
Alabama	Yes	No	No
Alaska	Yes	Not addressed in statute	Not addressed in statute
Arizona	Yes	Attorney	No
Arkansas	Yes	Not addressed in statute	Not addressed in statute
California	Yes	No	No
Colorado	Yes	Adoption exchange or licensed agency	No
Connecticut	Yes	Not addressed in statute	Not addressed in statute
Delaware	Yes	No	No
District of Columbia	Not addressed in statute	No	Not addressed in statute
Florida	Yes	Yes	No
Georgia	Yes	Yes	No
Hawaii	Not addressed in statute	Not addressed in statute	Not addressed in statute

STATE	BIRTH PARENT EXPENSES	PAYMENT FOR ARRANGING ADOPTION	PAYMENT FOR RELINQUISHING CHILD
Idaho	Yes	Not addressed in statute	No
Illinois	Yes	No	No
Indiana	Yes	Reasonable fees by licensed agency or county office	No
Iowa	Yes	Usual, necessary and commensurate with services rendered	No
Kansas	Yes	Reasonable legal or professional fees	No
Kentucky	Yes	No	No
Louisiana	Yes	No	No
Maine	Yes	Not addressed in statute	No
Maryland	Yes	No	No
Massachusetts	Not addressed in statute	Only authorized agents or employees of the Department of Social Services	No
Michigan	Yes	No	No
Minnesota	Yes	No	No
Mississippi	Yes	Licensed agency	Not addressed in statute
Missouri	Yes	No	No
Montana	Yes	No	No
Nebraska	Not addressed in statute	Not addressed in statute	Not addressed in statute
Nevada	Yes	Licensed agency	No
New Hampshire	Yes	Not addressed in statutes	No

STATE	BIRTH PARENT EXPENSES	PAYMENT FOR ARRANGING ADOPTION	PAYMENT FOR RELINQUISHING CHILD
New Jersey	Yes	Approved agency or person	No
New Mexico	Yes	Reasonable and actual fees for services	No
New York	Yes	Authorized agency	No
North Carolina	Yes	No	No
North Dakota	Yes	No	No
Ohio	Yes	No	No
Oklahoma	Yes	Licensed agency or Department of Social Services	No
Oregon	Yes	No	Not addressed in statute
Pennsy-lvania	Yes	No	No
Rhode Island	Not addressed in statute	Not addressed in statute	Not addressed in statute
South Carolina	Yes	Not addressed in statute	No
South Dakota	Yes	No	No
Tennessee	Yes	Licensed agency, licensed clinical social worker or Department of Social Services	No
Texas	Yes	Licensed agency	No
Utah	Yes	Not addressed in statutes	No

STATE	BIRTH PARENT EXPENSES	PAYMENT FOR ARRANGING ADOPTION	PAYMENT FOR RELINQUISHING CHILD
Vermont	Yes	No	No
Virginia	Yes	No	No
Washington	Yes	Not addressed in statute	No
West Virginia	Yes	No	No
Wisconsin	Yes	No	No
Wyoming	Not addressed in statute	Not addressed in statute	Not addressed in statute

Source: Child Welfare Information Gateway

APPENDIX 9:
QUALIFIED ADOPTION
EXPENSES (IRS FORM 8839)

Form **8839**	**Qualified Adoption Expenses**	OMB No. 1545-0074
Department of the Treasury Internal Revenue Service	▶ Attach to Form 1040 or 1040NR. ▶ See separate instructions.	20**06** Attachment Sequence No. **38**

Name(s) shown on return	Your social security number

Before you begin: See **Definitions** on page 1 of the instructions.

Part I | Information About Your Eligible Child or Children—You **must** complete this part. See page 2 of the instructions for details, including what to do if you need more space.

1	(a) Child's name		(b) Child's year of birth	Check if child was—			(f) Child's identifying number
	First	Last		(c) born **before** 1989 and disabled	(d) a child with special needs	(e) a foreign child	
Child 1				☐	☐	☐	
Child 2				☐	☐	☐	

Caution. If the child was a foreign child, see **Special rules** in the instructions for line 1, column (e), that begin on page 2, before you complete Part II or Part III. If you received **employer-provided adoption benefits,** complete Part III on the back next.

Part II | **Adoption Credit**

			Child 1		Child 2	
2	Maximum adoption credit per child	2	$10,960	00	$10,960	00
3	Did you file Form 8839 for a prior year for the same child? ☐ **No.** Enter -0-. ☐ **Yes.** See page 4 of the instructions for the amount to enter.	3				
4	Subtract line 3 from line 2	4				
5	**Qualified adoption expenses** (see page 4 of the instructions) **Caution.** Your qualified adoption expenses may not be equal to the adoption expenses you paid in 2006.	5				
6	Enter the **smaller** of line 4 or line 5	6				
7	Add the amounts on line 6. If zero, skip lines 8 through 11 and enter -0- on line 12	7				

8	Modified adjusted gross income (see page 4 of the instructions) . .	**8**	
9	Is line 8 more than $164,410?		
	☐ **No.** Skip lines 9 and 10, and enter -0- on line 11.		
	☐ **Yes.** Subtract $164,410 from line 8	**9**	
10	Divide line 9 by $40,000. Enter the result as a decimal (rounded to at least three places). Do not enter more than 1.000	**10**	✕ .
11	Multiply line 7 by line 10	**11**	
12	Subtract line 11 from line 7	**12**	
13	Credit carryforward from prior years (line 23 of your **Credit Carryforward Worksheet** on page 5 of the **2005** Form 8839 instructions)	**13**	
14	Add lines 12 and 13	**14**	
15	Enter the amount from Form 1040, line 46, or Form 1040NR, line 43 .	**15**	
16	**1040 filers:** Enter the total of any amounts from Form 1040, lines 47 through 51 and line 53; Form 8396, line 11; and Form 5695, line 12. } . . .	**16**	
	1040NR filers: Enter the total of any amounts from Form 1040NR, lines 44 through 46 and line 48; Form 8396, line 11; and Form 5695, line 12.)		
17	Subtract line 16 from line 15	**17**	
18	**Adoption credit.** Enter the smaller of line 14 or line 17 here and include on Form 1040, line 54, or Form 1040NR, line 49. Check box **b** on that line. If line 17 is smaller than line 14, you may have a credit carryforward (see page 4 of the instructions)	**18**	

For Paperwork Reduction Act Notice, see page 6 of the instructions. Cat. No. 22843L Form **8839** (2006)

The Law of Adoption

Form 8839 (2006)   Page **2**

Part III Employer-Provided Adoption Benefits

		Child 1		Child 2				
19	Maximum exclusion per child . . .	**19**	$10,960	00	$10,960	00		
20	Did you receive employer-provided adoption benefits for a prior year for the same child? ☐ **No.** Enter -0-. ☐ **Yes.** See page 4 of the instructions for the amount to enter. }	**20**						
21	Subtract line 20 from line 19	**21**						
22	Employer-provided adoption benefits you received in 2006. This amount should be shown in box 12 of your 2006 Form(s) W-2 with code **T** . . .	**22**						
23	Add the amounts on line 22						**23**	
24	Enter the **smaller** of line 21 or line 22. But if the child was a child with special needs and the adoption became final in 2006, enter the amount from line 21 .	**24**						
25	Add the amounts on line 24. If zero, skip lines 26 through 29, enter -0- on line 30, and go to line 31	**25**						
26	Modified adjusted gross income (from the worksheet on page 6 of the instructions)	**26**						
27	Is line 26 more than $164,410? ☐ **No.** Skip lines 27 and 28, and enter -0- on line 29. ☐ **Yes.** Subtract $164,410 from line 26	**27**						
28	Divide line 27 by $40,000. Enter the result as a decimal (rounded to at least three places). Do not enter more than 1.000 . . .	**28**	✕ .					
29	Multiply line 25 by line 28	**29**						
30	**Excluded benefits.** Subtract line 29 from line 25						**30**	
31	**Taxable benefits.** Is line 30 more than line 23? ☐ **No.** Subtract line 30 from line 23. Also, include this amount, if more than zero, on line 7 of Form 1040 or line 8 of Form 1040NR. On the dotted line next to line 7 of Form 1040 or line 8 of Form 1040NR, enter "AB." ☐ **Yes.** Subtract line 23 from line 30. Enter the result as a negative number. Reduce the total you would enter on line 7 of Form 1040 or line 8 of Form 1040NR by the amount on Form 8839, line 31. Enter the result on line 7 of Form 1040 or line 8 of Form 1040NR. Enter "SNE" on the dotted line next to the entry line. } . . .						**31**	

You may be able to claim the adoption credit in Part II on the front of this form if either of the following applies.
- The total adoption expenses you paid in 2006 were not fully reimbursed by your employer and the adoption became final in 2006 or earlier.
- You adopted a child with special needs and the adoption became final in 2006.

Form **8839** (2006)

APPENDIX 10:
TABLE OF STATE STATUTES GOVERNING CONSENT IN ADOPTION PROCEEDINGS

STATE	STATUTE
Alabama	Alabama Code §§ 26-10A-7 - 26-10A-14
Alaska	Alaska Stat. §§ 25.23.040 - 25.23-070
Arizona	Arizona Rev. Stat. §§ 8-106(A), (B), (D), (J); 8-107(A), (B)
Arkansas	Arkansas Ann. Code §§ 9-9-206 - 9-9-207
California	California Family Law §§ 8602 - 8606.5; 8700; 8801.3; 8814; 8814.5
Colorado	Colorado Rev. Stat. §§ 19-3-604; 19-5-103 - 104; 19-5-104(7)(a); 19-5-203; 19-5-207
Connecticut	Connecticut Gen. Stat. §§ 45a-715; 45a-717(d-g); 45a-719; 45a-724;
Delaware	Delaware Ann. Code Tit. 13 §§ 907; 908; 909; 1103(a); 1106(c)
District of Columbia	D.C. Ann. Code §§ 4-14-6(b); 4-1406(c)-(d), (f); 16-304; 16-304(a)
Florida	Florida Ann. Statutes §§ 63.062; 63.062(1)©; 63-064; 63-082
Georgia	Georgia Ann. Code §§ 19-8-4; 19-8-4(b); 19-8-5; 19-8-9(b); 19-8-10
Hawaii	Hawaii Rev. Stat. §§ 571-61; 578-2; 578-2(a); 578-2(a)(8); 578-2-(f)
Idaho	Idaho Code §§ 16-1504; 16-1506; 16-1515

STATE	STATUTE
Illinois	Ill. Cons. Stat. Ch. 750 §§50/8; 50/8(a); 50/8(b); 50/9; 50/10; 50/11; 50/12
Indiana	Indiana Ann. Code §§ 31-19-9-1; 31-19-9-2-2(d); 31-19-9-4; 31-19-9-8; 31-19-9-10
Iowa	Iowa Ann. Code §§ 600.7; 600A.4; 600A.4(2)(g); 600A.8;
Kansas	Kansas Ann. Statutes §§ 59-2114 - 59-2116; 59-2129; 59-2136(d); 59-2136(h)
Kentucky	Kentucky Rev. Stat. §§ 199.500; 199.502; 625.040
Louisiana	Louisiana Children's Code art. 1113; 1120; 1122 - 1123; 1130; 1147; 1193; 1195; 1245;
Maine	Maine Rev. Stat. Ann. Tit. 18-A, §§ 9-202; 9-302;
Maryland	Maryland Fam. Law §§ 5-3B-21(2); 5-3B-22; 5-338; 5-338(3); 5-339; 5-351
Massachusetts	Massachusetts Ann. Laws ch. 210 §§ 2, 3
Michigan	Michigan Comp. Laws Ann. §§ 710.29; 710.31; 710.37; 710.43; 710.44; 710.51(6)
Minnesota	Minnesota Ann. Stat. §§ 259.24, subd. 1, 2, 2a, 3, 5, 6a
Mississippi	Mississippi Ann. Code §§ 93-17-5; 93-17-7; 93-17-15
Missouri	Missouri Rev. Stat. §§ 453.030; 453.040
Montana	Montana Ann. Code §§ 42-2-301; 42-2-302; 42-2-303; 42-2-405; 42-2-408; 42-2-410
Nebraska	Nebraska Rev. Stat. §§ 43-104; 43-105; 43-106
Nevada	Nevada Rev. Stat. §§ 127.020; 127.040; 127.043; 127.053; 127.057; 127.070; 127.080
New Hampshire	New Hampshire Rev. Stat. §§ 170-B:3; 170-B:5; 170-B:7; 170-B:10; 170-B:12
New Jersey	New Jersey Ann. Stat. §§ 9:3-41; 9:3-41(a); 9:3-41(e); 9:3-45; 9:3-45(b)(4); 9:3-46; 9:3-49
New Mexico	New Mexico Ann. Stat. §§ 32A-5-17 - 32A-5-19; 32A-5-21; 32A-5-23
New York	New York Dom. Rel. Law §§ 111; 113; 115-b; Soc. Serv. Law § 384
North Carolina	North Carolina Gen. Stat. §§ 48-3-601 - 48-3-609
North Dakota	North Dakota Cent. Code §§ 14-15-05 - 14-15-08

STATE	STATUTE
Ohio	Ohio Rev. Code Ann. §§ 3107.06; 3107.07; 3107.08; 3107.08(A); 3107.084
Oklahoma	Oklahoma Ann. Stat. Tit. 10, §§ 7503-2.1 - 7503-2.4; 7503-2.6; 7503-2.7; 7505-4.2
Oregon	Oregon Ann. Stat. §§ 109.312 - 109.316; 109. 322 - 109.326; 109.328; 109.346; 418.270
Pennsylvania	Pennsylvania Cons. Stat. Ch. 23 §§ 2501 - 2504; 2511; 2711; 2711(d); 2713; 2714
Rhode Island	Rhode Island Gen. Laws §§ 15-7-5; 15-7-6; 15-7-7; 15-7-10; 15-7-21.1
South Carolina	South Carolina Ann. Code §§ 20-7-1690; 20-7-1695; 20-7-1700; 20-7-1705; 20-7-1720
South Dakota	South Dakota Codified Laws §§ 25-5A-4; 25-5A-16; 25-6-4; 25-6-5; 25-6-12; 25-6-21
Tennessee	Tennessee Ann. Code §§ 36-1-110; 36-1-111; 36-1-111(b); 36-1-112; 36-1-117;
Texas	Texas Fam. Code §§ 161.003 - 161.007; 161.103 - 161.106; 11.1035; 162.010; 162.011
Utah	Utah Ann. Code §§ 78-30-4; 78-30-6; 78-30-4.14; 78-30-4.17 - 78-30-4.21; 78-30-4.23
Vermont	Vermont Ann. Stat. Tit. 15A §§ 2-401; 2-402; 2-404; 2-405; 2-407; 2-408; 2-409
Virginia	Virginia Ann. Code §§ 63.2-1202; 63.2-1204; 63.2-1223; 63.2-1233; 63.2-1234; 63.2-1241
Washington	Washington Rev. Code §§ 26.33.080; 26.33.120; 26.33.160; 26.33.170
West Virginia	West Virginia Ann. Code §§ 48-22-301 - 48-22-305; 49-3-1
Wisconsin	Wisconsin Ann. Stat. §§ 48.41; 48.42; 48.46(2); 48.415; 48.837
Wyoming	Wyoming Ann. Stat. §§ 1-22-109; 1-22-109(d); 1-22-110;

Source: Child Welfare Information Gateway

APPENDIX 11:
TABLE OF STATE LAWS GOVERNING THE
RIGHTS OF PUTATIVE FATHERS

STATE	PUTATIVE FATHER REGISTRY	REGISTRY INFORMATION	PARTIES GIVEN ACCESS TO REGISTRY INFORMATION
Alabama	Yes	Address and SSN of any person adjudicated to be father or claiming paternity	Court handling adoption; any court upon request; any person upon court order for good cause
Alaska	No	Form acknowledging paternity; address and SSN of both parents and child	Not addressed in statutes
Arizona	Yes	Name and address of putative father and birth mother; child's birth date or expected birth date of child	Court; division; licensed adoption agency or attorney participating in direct placement adoption
Arkansas	Yes	Name/address and SSN of birth mother and person claiming TO be father; child's name and date/ location of birth, if known	Birth mother; child; registrant; Dept. of Human Services; attorneys involved in paternity, support or adoption litigation; Office of Child Support Enforcement
California	No	Not addressed in statutes	Not addressed in statutes

STATE	PUTATIVE FATHER REGISTRY	REGISTRY INFORMATION	PARTIES GIVEN ACCESS TO REGISTRY INFORMATION
Colorado	No	Not addressed in statutes	Not addressed in statutes
Connecticut	No	Name and address of putative father and birth mother; birth date or expected birth date of child	Within 5 days, copy of father's claim is sent to birth mother
Delaware	Yes	None specified in statutes	Court or person designated by court; mother; authorized agency; licensed child placement agency; child support enforcement agency; party to case or attorney; other State paternity registry
District Of Columbia	No	Not addressed in statutes	Not addressed in statutes
Florida	Yes	Name, address, date of birth and physical description of putative father and mother; Date, place and location of conception; name, date and place of child's birth or estimated date of birth, if known	Petitioner and court in a termination of parental rights or adoption proceeding
Georgia	Yes	Name, address and SSN of biological but not legal father; date of registration	State agency or department; licensed child placement agency; member of georgia bar
Hawaii	No	Not addressed in statutes	Not addressed in statutees
Idaho	Yes	Name and address of putative father and birth mother; child's date of birth or expected date of birth	Identities of putative fathers can only be released pursuant to statutory procedures

STATE	PUTATIVE FATHER REGISTRY	REGISTRY INFORMATION	PARTIES GIVEN ACCESS TO REGISTRY INFORMATION
Illinois	Yes	Name, address, SSN and date of birth of putative father and birth mother; name, gender, date and place of birth of child; date of putative father's registration	Prospective adoptive parents; birth mother; child welfare agency; attorney representing party
Indiana	Yes	Name, address, SSN and date of birth of putative father and birth mother; child's name and date of birth, if known; date of registration; name of attorney or agency requesting search	Registrant; birth mother; child; any party or attorney in pending adoption; attorney representing prosepctive parents; licensed child placement agency; court presiding over pending adoption
Iowa	Yes	Name, address SSN of putative father and birth mother; name, date and location of birth of child, if known	Birth mother; court; Department of Human Services; attorney for any party to adoption ot termination proceeding; Child Support Recovery Unit; any other person upon court order
Kansas	No	Not addressed in statutes	Not addressed in statutes
Kentucky	No	Not addressed in statutes	Not addressed in statutes
Louisiana	Yes	Names and addresses of any person adjudicated to be father; or who filed declaration of paternity; or who filed acknowledgment, legitimation or judgment of filiation	Any court; an authorized agency; any person upon court order

STATE	PUTATIVE FATHER REGISTRY	REGISTRY INFORMATION	PARTIES GIVEN ACCESS TO REGISTRY INFORMATION
Maine	No	Voluntary acknowledgment of paternity signed by both mother and putative father	Not addressed in statutes
Maryland	No	Not addressed in statutes	Not addressed in statutes
Massachusetts	No	Not addressed in statutes	Notice of the filing of a claim of paternity is sent to the birth mother
Michigan	No	Name and address of putative father and birth mother	Sent to birth mother
Minnesota	Yes	Name, address, SSN and date of birth of putative father and birth mother; certified copy of court order from another State adjudicating putative father to be father; child's name, gender, date and place of birth, if known	Person who is required to search registry prior to adoption placement; mother; public authority responsible for child support enforcement; attorney representing birth mother or adoptive parents
Mississippi	No	Not addressed in statutes	Not addressedin statutes
Missouri	Yes	Name, and address of any person adjudicated by a court to be the father and who filed with the registry before or after child's birth	Any court; an authorized agency; any other person upon court order; Department of Social Services; child placement agency; child's parents; an intermediary (attorney, physician or parents' clergy)
Montana	Yes	Name, address, SSN and date of birth of putative father and birth mother; chld's name and place of birth, or expected date and location; date of registration	Department representative; adoption agency; prospective adoptive parents or attorney; woman who is subject of registration

STATE	PUTATIVE FATHER REGISTRY	REGISTRY INFORMATION	PARTIES GIVEN ACCESS TO REGISTRY INFORMATION
Nebraska	Yes	Name and addresses of any person who was adjudicated to be the father; or who filed a paternity claim or a notice of intent to claim paternity and obtain custody with registry	Department of Correctional Services; Department of Health and Human Services; any person authorized by law or upon court order
Nevada	No	Not addressed in statutes	Not addressed in statutes
New Hampshire	Yes	Not addressed in statutes	Not addressed in statutes
New Jersey	No	Not addressed in statutes	Not addressed in statutes
New Mexico	Yes	Name and address of any person adjudicated to be the father; or who has filed a paternity claim or acknowled-gment, or a notice of intent to claim paternity	Any court; Department of Health; petitioner's attorney; agency; birth mother; any other person upon court order
New York	Yes	Name and address of any person adjudicated by court to be the father; or who has filed a notice of intent to claim paternity or acknowledgment	Any court; an authorized agency; any other person upon a court order
North Carolina	No	Not addressed in statutes	Not addressed in statutes
North Dakota	No	Not addressed in statutes	Not addressed in statutes

STATE	PUTATIVE FATHER REGISTRY	REGISTRY INFORMATION	PARTIES GIVEN ACCESS TO REGISTRY INFORMATION
Ohio	Yes	Putative father's name, address and phone number; birth mother's name; date of receipt of form	Birth mother; agency; attorney arranging adoption of child
Oklahoma	Yes	Name, address, SSN and date or birth of putative father and birth mother; child's name, date and place of birth or expected birth; date father registered; name of person doing search	Any court; an authorized agency; any person deemed necessary by Department of Human Services; any other person who can show good cause
Oregon	No	A notice may be sent to the Center for Health Statistics including full name and address of child; date and place of child's birth or expected birth; full names and addresses of child's parents	Information in notice shall be provided to persons whose names appear in notice; and to persons or agencies with a legitimate interest including parties to adoption of child
Pennsylvania	No	Not addressed in statutes	Not addressed in statutes
Rhode Island	No	Not addressed in statutes	Not addressed in statutes
South Carolina	No	Not addressed in statutes	Not addressed in statutes
South Dakota	No	Not addressed in statutes	Not addressed in statutes
Tennessee	Yes	Name and address of putative father, child, and birth mother; names of persons who have filed acknowledgment or notice of intent to claim paternity; names of persons who have been adjudicated to be father	Any notice of intent to claim paternity may be used as evidence by any other party in any proceeding in which the parentage of a child may be relevant

STATE	PUTATIVE FATHER REGISTRY	REGISTRY INFORMATION	PARTIES GIVEN ACCESS TO REGISTRY INFORMATION
Texas	Yes	Not addressed in statutes	Birth mother; court; authorized agency; licensed child placement agency; child support enforcement agency; attorney involved in case; Registry of another State
Utah	No	Not addressed in statutes	Not addressed in statutes
Vermont	No	Not addressed in statutes	Not addressed in statutes
Virginia	No	Not addressed in statutes	Not addressed in statutes
Washington	No	Acknowledg-ment of paternity may be filed with state registrat of vital statistics and must be in a record; signed by the mother and man seeking to establish paternity; state that child does not have another presumed or adjuicated father; and state whether there has been genetic testing and whether claim of paternity is consistent with result of testing	State registrar of vital statistics may release information relating to acknowledgment of paternity to a signatory of the acknowledgment or their attorney of record; the courts; agencies operating a child support program; and agencies involvedin a dependency determination for a child named in the acknowledgment
West Virginia	No	Not addressed in statutes	Not addressed in statutes
Wisconsin	No	Declaration may be filed which must include the name and address of the putative father and birth mother; month and year of child's birth or expected birth; Statement that	Declaration sent to the birth mother

STATE	PUTATIVE FATHER REGISTRY	REGISTRY INFORMATION	PARTIES GIVEN ACCESS TO REGISTRY INFORMATION
		the individual has reason to believe he may be the child's father	
Wyoming	Yes	Name and address of any person who has been adjudicated to be the father; who has filed a notice of intent to claim paternity with the registry before or after child's birth; or who has filed an acknowledgment of paternity with the registry	Any court; any auithorized agency; any person upon court order

Source: Child Welfare Information Gateway

APPENDIX 12:
TABLE OF STATE INFANT SAFE HAVEN LAWS

STATE	AGE	WHO MAY RELINQUISH INFANT	WHO MAY RECEIVE INFANT/IMMUNITY	RESPONSI-BILITIES OF RECEIVER	PROTECTION FOR RELINQUISHING PARENT	EFFECT ON PARENTAL RIGHTS
Alabama	72 Hours or younger	Parent	EMS provider in licensed hospital/immunity	Protect health of child and notify Department of Human Resources	Affirmative defense to prosecution for nonsupport, abandonment or endangering welfare of child	Department assumes control and custody of child
Alaska	Not addressed in statutes	Not addressed in statutes	Not addressed in statutes	Not addressed in statutes	Not addressed in statutes	Not addressed in statutes
Arizona	72 Hours or younger	Parent or agent of parent	Firefighter or EMS on duty; health care institution; private child welfare agency/immunity	Notify child protective services; offer information and referrals	Anonymity; not guilty of abuse	Not addressed in statutes
Arkansas	30 Days or younger	Parent or person designated by parent	Medical provider; law enforcement agency/immunity	Protect health of child and notify Division of Children and Family Services	Affirmative defense to prosecution for endangering welfare of child	Department will innitiate dependency action for child placement

STATE	AGE	WHO MAY RELINQUISH INFANT	WHO MAY RECEIVE INFANT/IMMUNITY	RESPONSI-BILITIES OF RECEIVER	PROTECTION FOR RELINQUISHING PARENT	EFFECT ON PARENTAL RIGHTS
California	72 hours or younger	Parent or legal custodian	Public or private hospital; any designated location/immunity	Provide medical care and ankle bracelet to child; notify child protective services	Immunity from prosecution for abandonment, failure to provide and desertion	Dependency petition filed; parent has 14 days to reclaim child
Colorado	72 hours or younger	Parent	Fire station; hospital/immunity	Protect health of child; notify law enforcement and county	Affirmative defense to prosecution;	Child placed for adoption; termination of parental rights
Connecticut	30 days or younger	Parent or agent of parent	Hospital emergency room/ not addressed in statutes	Take custody; notify department within 24 hours	Confidentiality; no violation of child abandonment statute	Department assumes custody; parent may submit request for reunification
Delaware	14 days of younrger	Any person	Hospital emergency dept./Immunity	Take custody; notify State police	Anonymity; defense to prosecution for abandonment or endangering welfare of child	Irrevocable consent to termination of parental rights unless rights exercised within 30 days

STATE	AGE	WHO MAY RELINQUISH INFANT	WHO MAY RECEIVE INFANT/IMMUNITY	RESPONSI-BILITIES OF RECEIVER	PROTECTION FOR RELINQUISHING PARENT	EFFECT ON PARENTAL RIGHTS
District of Columbia	Not addressed in statutes	Not addressed in statutes	Not addressed in statutes	Not addressed in statutes	Not addressed in statutes	Not addressed in statutes
Florida	3 days old or younger	Parent	Hiospital; EMS station; fire station/immunity	Provide medical care; contact child placement agency; report suspected abuse or neglect	Anonymity; immunity from prosecution for abandonment unless abuse or neglect	Prsumption of consent to terminate parental rights; parent may reclaim prior to termination
Georgia	Not more than 1 week old	Mother	Hospital; infirmary; health center; birth center/immunity	Admit child; notify Department of Human Resources	No prosecution for cruelty	Department will take physical custody
Hawaii	Not addressed in statutes	Not addressed in statutes	Not addressed in statutes	Not addressed in statutes	Not addressed in statutes	Not addressed in statutes
Idaho	30 days or younger	Custodial parent	Hospital; physician; nurse; midwife; physician assistant; EMS/immunity	Protect child's health and safety; notify peace officer; take temporary custody	Confidentiality; immunity from prosecution for abandonment and neglect	Placement for adoption; petition to terminate parental rights; parent may reclaim prior to termination

STATE	AGE	WHO MAY RELINQUISH INFANT	WHO MAY RECEIVE INFANT/IMMUNITY	RESPONSI-BILITIES OF RECEIVER	PROTECTION FOR RELINQUISHING PARENT	EFFECT ON PARENTAL RIGHTS
Illinois	72 hours or younger	Biological parent	Hospital; police or fire station; emergency medical facility/immunity	Notify child protective services; provide medical care; take child to hospital; hospital must evaluate for neglect or abuse and take temporary custody	Anonymity if no evidence of abuse; relinquishment not considered abandonment or endangerment	Presumption of consent to termination of parental rights; may petition to reclaim child prior to termination
Indiana	45 days or younger	Parent; any person	EMS provider/ immunity	Take custody; protect child's health and safety; notify child protection services	Anonymity; defense to prosecution for abandonment or neglect	Child protection services assumes custody
Iowa	14 days or younger	Parent; person authorized by parent	Institutional health facility/immunity	Take custody; protect child's health and safety; notify department	Anonymity; confidentiality; immunity from criminal or civil proceedings	Petition to terminate parental rights; parent may request custody prior to termination

STATE	AGE	WHO MAY RELINQUISH INFANT	WHO MAY RECEIVE INFANT/IMMUNITY	RESPONSI-BILITIES OF RECEIVER	PROTECTION FOR RELINQUISHING PARENT	EFFECT ON PARENTAL RIGHTS
Kansas	45 days or younger	Parent; legal custodian	Fire station; city or county health dept.; Medical care facility	Take custody; protect child's health and safety; notify law enforcement	Immune from prosecution for abandonment if no harm to baby	Petition for termination of parental rights; expedited hearing
Kentucky	72 hours or younger	Parent; any person	EMS provider; police; firefighter/immunity	Provide medical care; notify Department of Community Based Services	Anonymity; confidentiality; no investigation for abandonment	Placement with foster family; petition for termination of parental rights; parent may reclaim child prior to termination
Louisiana	30 days or younger	Parent	Designated emergency care facility/immunity	Notify department immediately; provide parent with information	Relinquishment is not a criminal act of neglect, abandonment, cruelty or crime against child	Department takes custody; parent can reclaim within 30 days of relinquishment
Maine	Less than 31 days	Any person	Law enforcement officer; emergency room; medical services provider; hospital staff/immunity	Notify the department; request information	Affirmative defense to prosecution for abandonment; confidentiality	Not addressed in statutes

STATE	AGE	WHO MAY RELINQUISH INFANT	WHO MAY RECEIVE INFANT/IMMUNITY	RESPONSI-BILITIES OF RECEIVER	PROTECTION FOR RELINQUISHING PARENT	EFFECT ON PARENTAL RIGHTS
Maryland	Within 3 days of birth	Mother; person with approval of mother	Responsible adult; hospital or other designated facility/immunity	Take child to hospital; hospital shall notify department within 24 hours	Immunity from civil or criminal liability	Not addressed in statutes
Massachusetts	7 days or less	Parent	Hospital; police department; fire station/immunity not addressed	Immediately notify department; solicit information from parent	Relinquishment shall not constitute finding of abuse; neglect or abandonment	Placement in foster care; petition to terminate parental rights
Michigan	72 hours or younger	Parent	Fire department; hospital; police station/immunity	Take custody; provide medical care; report suspected abusse	Confidentiality; affirmative defense to prosecution for injury or abandonment	Parent has 28 days to petition for custody or petition to terminate parental rights w/o notice
Minnesota	72 hours or younger	Mother; person with mother's approval	Employee at licensed hospital/immunity	Inform local child welfare agency within 24 hours	No prosecution for leaving infant; parent not required to provide information	Social services agency takes custody; no requirement to attempt reunification with parent

STATE	AGE	WHO MAY RELINQUISH INFANT	WHO MAY RECEIVE INFANT/IMMUNITY	RESPONSI-BILITIES OF RECEIVER	PROTECTION FOR RELINQUISHING PARENT	EFFECT ON PARENTAL RIGHTS
Mississippi	72 hours or younger	Parent	Licensed hospital emergency department; licensed adoption agency/immunity	Protect child's health and safety; notify department	Affirmative defense to prosecution for abandonment, neglect or exposure of child	Department of Human Services assumes custody and control of child
Missouri	No more than 30 days	Biological parent; person acting on parent's behalf	Hospital staff; firefighter or emergency medical technician; law enforcement officer/immunity	Take custody and transport to hospital; provide medical treatment; notify division of family services	No prosecution for abandonment and endangerment for child under 5 days old or younger; affirmative defense if child 6 to 30 days old	Child made ward of court; implied consent relinquishment of parental rights; must reclaim within 30 days of public notice
Montana	No more than 30 days old	Parent; an individual	On duty employee of fire department; hospital or law enforcement agency/immunity	Protect child's health and safety; notify department; report suspected abuse	Confidentiality; no prosecution for abandonment based on relinquishment	Child released for adoption; parent has 60 days to petition court to regain custody

STATE	AGE	WHO MAY RELINQUISH INFANT	WHO MAY RECEIVE INFANT/IMMUNITY	RESPONSI-BILITIES OF RECEIVER	PROTECTION FOR RELINQUISHING PARENT	EFFECT ON PARENTAL RIGHTS
Nebraska	Not addressed in statutes	Not addressed in statutes	Not addressed in statutes	Not addressed in statutes	Not addressed in statutes	Not addressed in statutes
Nevada	30 days or less	Parent	Hospital; obstetric center; emergency medical care center; fire station; law enforcement agency/immunity	Maintain health and safety of child; notify child welfare agency within 24 hours	Anonymity; no prosecution for abandonment, abuse, neglect or endangering child	Parent presumed to have consent to termination of parental rights
New Hampshire	Not more than 7 days old	Parent	Hospital; church with attendee; police of fire station/immunity	Protect health and safety of child; notify department and law enforcement within 24 hours	Anonymity	Department assumes temporary care and control of child
New Jersey	30 days or less	Parent; any person	Police station; hospital emergency dept./Immunity	Transport child to hospital; hospital shall take custody, treat and notify Division of Youth and Family Services within first business day of possession	Anonymity; affirmative defense to prosecution for abandonment	Division will place child for adoption as soon as possible; no requirement to attempt reunification with parent

STATE	AGE	WHO MAY RELINQUISH INFANT	WHO MAY RECEIVE INFANT/IMMUNITY	RESPONSI-BILITIES OF RECEIVER	PROTECTION FOR RELINQUISHING PARENT	EFFECT ON PARENTAL RIGHTS
New Mexico	90 days or less	Any person	Staff of licensed hospital or health care clinic/immunity	Provide necessary medical care; notify department within 24 hours	Anonymity; confidentiality; no prosecution for abandonment or abuse	Department takes custody; parent has 30 days to seek reunification
New York	Not more than 5 days old	Any person	An appropriate person/immunity not addressed	Not addressed in statutes	Affirmative defense to prosecution for abandonment or endangering welfare of child	Not addressed in statutes
North Carolina	Less than 7 days old	Parent	Health care provider; law enforcement officer; social services worker; EMS worker; any adult/immunity	Protect child's health and well-being; notify Department of Social Serivces or law enforcement agency	Anonymity; no prosecution for abandonment or failure to support	Provider takes temporary custody of child
North Dakota	Less than 1 year old	Parent; agent of parent	Licensed hospital/immunity	Notify department within 24 hours; request/provide information to parent	Anonymity; no prosecution for abuse, neglect or abandonment	Parental participation in court action if rights not terminated yet

STATE	AGE	WHO MAY RELINQUISH INFANT	WHO MAY RECEIVE INFANT/IMMUNITY	RESPONSI-BLITIES OF RECEIVER	PROTECTION FOR RELINQUISHING PARENT	EFFECT ON PARENTAL RIGHTS
Ohio	Less than 72 hours	Parent	EMS worker; hospital employee; peace officer/immunity	Protect child's health and safety; notify Children's Services Agency; request/provide information	Anonymity; no prosecution for relinquishment	Child considered deserted or neglected child; parent seeking reunification must undergo DNA testing
Oklahoma	7 days or younger	Parent	Police station; fire station; CPS agency; hospital or medical facility/immunity	Protect child's health; notify department; request/provide information	Anonymity; no prosecution for abandonment or neglect	Department provides information about reunification
Oregon	30 days or younger	Parent	Hospital; birthing center; physician's office; sheriff's office; police station; fire station/immunity	Receive child; notify State Office for Services to Children within 24 hours	Anonymity; affirmative defense to prosecution for abandonment	Child considered abandoned; department has protective custody

STATE	AGE	WHO MAY RELINQUISH INFANT	WHO MAY RECEIVE INFANT/IMMUNITY	RESPONSI-BILITIES OF RECEIVER	PROTECTION FOR RELINQUISHING PARENT	EFFECT ON PARENTAL RIGHTS
Pennsylvania	Less than 28 days	Parent	Hospital; health care provider/immunity	Take custody of child; perform medical evaluation; immediately notify county agency and law enforcement	Parent into criminally liable	Not addressed in statutes
Rhode Island	30 Days or younger	Parent; person acting at direction of parent	Hospital; medical emergency facility; fire station; police station/immunity	Provide medical care; notify department; offer information	Confidentiality; immunity from prosecution for abandonment	Department has protective custody; petition for termination of parental rights filed in 90 days unless parent reclaims child
South Carolina	Not more than 30 days	Parent; person directed by parent	Hospital; hospital outpatient facility/immunity	Protect health and safety of child; request and provide information; notify department by close of first business day	Anonymity; confidentiality; immunity from prosecution for any criminal offense if child unharmed	Department takes legal custody; petition to terminate filed within 48 hours; parent seeking reunification must assert parental rights at first hearing

STATE	AGE	WHO MAY RELINQUISH INFANT	WHO MAY RECEIVE INFANT/ IMMUNITY	RESPONSI-BILITIES OF RECEIVER	PROTECTION FOR RELINQUISHING PARENT	EFFECT ON PARENTAL RIGHTS
South Dakota	Less than 60 days	Parent	Health care facility or clinic; law enforcement officer; EMS technician; firefighter; child placement agency/immunity	Protect child's health; notify the Department of Social Services	Anonymity; relinquishment not consider crime if child unharmed	After 14 days, child becomes ward of State and parental rights terminated; non-relinquishing parent has 30 days to file for custody
Tennessee	72 hours or younger	Mother	Hospital; birthing center; community health clinic; outpatient walk-in clinic/immunity	Protect child's health and safety; request and provide information; notify department wtihin 24 hours	Confidentiality; immunity from criminal prosecution if child unharmed	Department of Children's Services assumes custody; notice to putative father; failure of mother to contact within 90 days is grounds for termination

STATE	AGE	WHO MAY RELINQUISH INFANT	WHO MAY RECEIVE INFANT/ IMMUNITY	RESPONSI-BILITIES OF RECEIVER	PROTECTION FOR RELINQUISHING PARENT	EFFECT ON PARENTAL RIGHTS
Texas	60 days or younger	Parent	EMS provider; hospital; child placement agency/immunity	Protect child's health and safety; notify department by close of first business day	Anonymity; affirmative defense to prosecution for abandonment or endangerment	Department of Protective Services assumes custody of child
Utah	72 hours or younger	Parent; parent's designee	Hospital/ immunity	Provide necessary medical care; notify Division of Child and Family Services within 24 hours; prepare birth certificate for child if parentage unknown	Anonymity; affirmative defense to criminal liability for abandonment or neglect	Placement in potential adoptive home; petition to terminate parental rights filed within 10 days; father has 2 weeks to establish paternity
Vermont	Not addressed in statutes	Not addressed in statutes	Not addressed in statutes	Not addressed in statutes	Not addressed in statutes	Not addressed in statutes
Virginia	Within first 14 days	Parent	Hospital with 24 hour emergency services; rescue squad with ems/immunity	Not addressed in statutes	Affirmative defense to prosecution for abuse, neglect, cruelty or endangerment	Department takes custody; arranges placement; institutes termination proceeding

STATE	AGE	WHO MAY RELINQUISH INFANT	WHO MAY RECEIVE INFANT/ IMMUNITY	RESPONSI-BILITIES OF RECEIVER	PROTECTION FOR RELINQUISHING PARENT	EFFECT ON PARENTAL RIGHTS
Washington	Less than 72 hours	Parent	Hospital staff; fire station staff/immunity	Notify child protective services within 24 hours	Anonymity; no criminal liability for abandonment	Protective services assumees custody
West Virginia	Less than 30 days	Parent	Hospital; health care facility/ immunity not addressed	Protect child's health and safety; notify child protective services	Anonymity; affirmative defense to prosecution	Department assumes custody; child eligible for adoption
Wisconsin	72 hours or younger	Parent	Law enforcement officer; EMS technician; hospital staff member; sheriff's office; police station; fire station/immunity	Protect the child's health and safety; deliver child to intake worker within 24 hours; file birth certificate for child within 5 days	Anonymity; immunity from criminal and civil liability for abandonment or neglect	Court may grant involuntary termination of parental rights on grounds custody has been relinquished

STATE	AGE	WHO MAY RELINQUISH INFANT	WHO MAY RECEIVE INFANT/ IMMUNITY	RESPONSI- BILITIES OF RECEIVER	PROTECTION FOR RELINQUISHING PARENT	EFFECT ON PARENTAL RIGHTS
Wyoming	14 days or younger	Parent; parent's designee	Fire station; police department; sheriff's office; hospital; facility designated by department/ immunity	Provide emergency medical care; deliver child to hospital; notify child protective services agency within 24 hours	Anonymity; relinquishment does not constitute child abuse; affirmative defense to criminal liability for abandonment or neglect	Child protective agency assumes custody; placement in potential adoptive home; petition for termination of parental rights filed within 3 months

Source: child welfare information gateway

APPENDIX 13:
TABLE OF STATE STATUTES GOVERNING INTESTATE INHERITANCE RIGHTS OF ADOPTED CHILDREN

STATE	STATUTE
Alabama	Alabama Code §§ 43.8.48; 26.10A.29
Alaska	Alaska Statutes §§ 25.23.130; 13.12.114
Arizona	Arizona Revised Statutes §§ 8-117; 14-2114
Arkansas	Arkansas Ann. Code § 9-9-215
California	California Probate Code §§ 6450; 6451
Colorado	Colorado Revised Statutes §§ 15-11-103(6)-(7); 15-11-115
Connecticut	Connecticut Gen. Statutes §§ 45a-731(1)-(3), (6), (8)
Delaware	Delaware Ann. Code Tit. 13 § 920
District of Columbia	D.C. Ann. Code § 16-312
Florida	Florida Ann. Statutes §§ 63.172; 732.108
Georgia	Georgia Ann. Code § 19-8-19
Hawaii	Hawaii Revised Statutes §§ 578-16; 560:2-114
Idaho	Idaho Ann. Code §§ 16-1509; 16-1509
Illinois	Illinois Cons. Stat. Tit. 755, §§ 5/2-4(a), (b), (d)
Indiana	Indiana Ann. Code § 29-1-2-8
Iowa	Iowa Ann. Statutes § 633.223

STATE	STATUTE
Kansas	Kansas Ann. Statutes § 59-2118
Kentucky	Kentucky Revised Statutes § 199.520
Louisiana	Louisiana Children's Code Art. 1240; 1256(C)
Maine	Maine Revised Statutes Tit. 18-A, §§9-105; 2-109
Maryland	Maryland Family Law § 5-308; Est. & Trusts § 1-207
Massachusetts	Massachusetts Ann. Laws Chapter 210, §7
Michigan	Michigan Comp. Laws §§ 710.60; 700.2114
Minnesota	Minnesota Ann. Statutes § 259.59
Mississippi	Mississippi Ann. Code § 93-17-13
Missouri	Missouri Ann. Statutes §§ 453.090; 474.060
Montana	Montana Ann. Code § 72-2-124
Nebraska	Nebraska Revised Statutes §§ 43-111; 30-2309
Nevada	Nevada Revised Statutes § 127.160
New Hampshire	New Hampshire Revised Statutes § 170-B:25
New Jersey	New Jersey Ann. Statutes § 9:3-50
New Mexico	New Mexico Ann. Statutes §§ 45-2-114; 32A-5-37
New York	New York Domestic Relations Law § 117
North Carolina	North Carolina General Statutes § 48-1-106
North Dakota	North Dakota Cent. Code § 14-15-14
Ohio	Ohio Revised Code § 3107.15
Oklahoma	Oklahoma Ann. Statutes Tit. 10, § 7505-6.5
Oregon	Oregon Revised Statutes § 112.175
Pennsylvania	Pennsylvania Cons. Statutes Tit. 20, § 2108
Rhode Island	Rhode Island General Laws § 15-7-17
South Carolina	South Carolina Ann. Laws §§ 20-7-1576; 20-7-1770; 62-2-109
South Dakota	South Dakota Ann. Code § 29A-2-114
Tennessee	Tennessee Ann. Code § 36-1-121
Texas	Texas Prob. Code § 40; Fam. Code § 162.507

STATE	STATUTE
Utah	Utah Ann. Code § 75-2-114
Vermont	Vermont Ann. Statutes. Tit. 15A, §§ 1-104; 1-105
Virginia	Virginia Ann. Code § 64.1-5.1
Washington	Washington Rev. Code §§ 11.04.085; 26.33.260
West Virginia	West Virginia Ann. Code § 48-22-703
Wisconsin	Wisconsin Ann. Statutes § 854.20
Wyoming	Wyoming Ann. Statutes § 2-4-107

Source: Child Welfare Information Gateway

GLOSSARY

Abandonment by Parents—Refers to a situation where the child's parents have willfully forsaken all parental rights, obligations and claims to the child, as well as all control over and possession of the child, without intending to transfer, or without transferring, these rights to any specific person(s).

Abuse and Neglect—Physical, sexual and/or emotional maltreatment.

Acknowledgement—A formal declaration of one's signature before a notary public.

Adoptee—An adopted person.

Adoption—A court action in which an adult assumes legal and other responsibilities for another, usually a minor.

Adoption Agency—An organization, usually licensed by the State, that provides services to birth parents, adoptive parents, and children who need families. Agencies may be public or private, secular or religious, for profit or nonprofit.

Adoption Assistance—Monthly or one-time only subsidy payments to help adoptive parents raise children with special needs pursuant to the Adoption Assistance and Child Welfare Act of 1980 (P.L. 96-272) which provided Federal funding for children eligible under title IV-E of the Social Security Act; States also fund monthly payments for children with special needs who are not eligible for federally-funded subsidy payments.

Adoption Attorney—A legal professional who has experience with filing, processing, and finalizing adoptions in a court having jurisdiction.

Adoption Benefits—Compensation to workers through employer-sponsored programs. Some examples of such benefits are financial assistance or monetary reimbursement for the expenses of adopting a child, or provision of "parental" or "family" leave.

Adoption Consultant—Anyone who helps with the placement of a child, but specifically someone who makes it his or her private business to facilitate adoptions.

Adoption Disruption—The interruption of an adoption prior to finalization—sometimes called a "failed adoption" or a "failed placement".

Adoption Dissolution—The interruption or "failure" of an adoption after finalization that requires court action.

Adoption Exchange—An organization which recruits adoptive families for children with special needs.

Adoption Facilitator—Individual whose business involves connecting birth parents and prospective adoptive parents for a fee.

Adoption Cancellation Insurance—Insurance which protects against financial loss which can be incurred after a birthmother changes her mind and decides not to place her child for adoption.

Adoption Petition—The legal document through which prospective parents request the court's permission to adopt a specific child.

Adoption Placement—The point at which a child begins to live with prospective adoptive parents but before the adoption is finalized.

Adoption Plan—Birth parents' decisions to allow their child to be placed for adoption.

Adoption Reversal—Reclaiming of a child by birth parent(s) who have had a subsequent change of heart.

Adoption Subsidies—Federal or State adoption benefits—also known as adoption assistance—designed to help offset the short and long term costs associated with adopting children who need special services.

Adoption Tax Credits—Non-refundable credit which reduces taxes owed by adoptive parents who claim adoption expense reimbursement, which may be claimed on Federal taxes and in some states with similar legislation, on state taxes.

Adoption Tax Exclusions—IRS provisions in the Federal tax code which allow adoptive parents to exclude cash or other adoption benefits for qualifying adoption expenses received from a private-sector employer when computing the family's adjusted gross income for tax purposes.

Adoption Triad—The three major parties in an adoption: birth parents, adoptive parents, and adopted child.

Adult Adoption—The adoption of a person over the age of majority.

Adult Member of Prospective Adoptive Parents' Household—Refers to an individual, other than the prospective adoptive parent, over the age of 18, whose principal or only residence is the home of the prospective adoptive parents.

Affidavit—A sworn or affirmed statement made in writing and signed; if sworn, it is notarized.

Agency Adoption—Adoptive placements made by licensed organizations that screen prospective adoptive parents and supervise the placement of children in adoptive homes until the adoption is finalized.

Attestation—The act of witnessing an instrument in writing at the request of the party making the same, and subscribing it as a witness.

Birth Parent—A child's biological parent.

Black Market Adoption—An adoption in which one or more parties make a profit from a child placement, as opposed to receiving payment for providing counseling, location, or other services.

Boarder Babies—Infants abandoned in hospitals because of the parents' inability to care for them.

Bonding—The process of developing lasting emotional ties with one's immediate caregivers.

Certification—The approval process that takes place to ensure, insofar as possible, that adoptive or foster parents are suitable, dependable, and responsible.

Closed Adoption—An adoption that involves total confidentiality and sealed records.

Competent Authority—A court or governmental agency of a foreign country having jurisdiction and authority to make decisions in matters of child welfare, including adoption.

Confidentiality—The legally required process of keeping identifying or other significant information secret; the principle of ethical practice which requires social workers and other professional not to disclose information about a client without the client's consent.

Consent to Adopt—Legal permission for the adoption to proceed.

Constitution—The fundamental principles of law that frame a governmental system.

Constitutional Right—Refers to the individual liberties granted by the constitution of a state or the federal government.

Co-residency—Evidence that the adoptive parent and child reside together in a familial relationship under which the adoptive parent asserts parental control, e.g., provides financial support, supervision, living arrangement in adoptive parent's home, etc.

Custody—The care, control, and maintenance of a child.

De Facto Adoption—A legal agreement to adopt a child according to the laws of a particular State which will result in a legal adoption process once the adoption petition is filed with the appropriate court; an equitable adoption.

Decree of Adoption—A legal order that finalizes an adoption.

Desertion by Parents—Refers to a situation where the parents have willfully forsaken their child and have refused to carry out their parental rights and obligations.

Disappearance of Parents—Refers to a situation where both parents have unaccountably or inexplicably passed out of the child's life, their whereabouts are unknown, there is no reasonable hope of their reappearance and there has been a reasonable effort to locate them.

Disclosure—The release or transmittal of previously hidden or unknown information.

Disruption—The term disruption is used to describe an adoption that ends before it is legally finalized.

Dissolution—The term dissolution is used to describe an adoption that fails after finalization.

Due Process Rights—All rights which are of such fundamental importance as to require compliance with due process standards of fairness and justice.

Equitable Adoption—The legal process used in some states to establish inheritance rights of a child, when the prospective adoptive parent had entered into an oral contract to adopt the child and the child was placed with the parent but the adoption was not finalized before the parent died.

Employer Assistance—Adoption benefits provided to employees by employers which may include direct cash assistance for adoption expenses, reimbursement of approved adoption expenses, paid or unpaid leave and resource and referral services.

Finalization—The final legal step in the adoption process when the adoptive parents become the child's legal parents.

Foster-Adoption—A child placement in which the birth parents' rights have not yet been severed by the court or in which birth parents are appealing the court's decision but foster parents agree to adopt the child if and when parental rights are terminated.

Foster Children—Children who have been placed in the State's or county's legal custody because their birth parents were deemed abusive, neglectful, or otherwise unable to care for them.

Foster Parents—State or county licensed adults who provide a temporary home for children whose birth parents are unable to care for them.

Fraud—A false representation of a matter of fact, whether by words or by conduct, by false or misleading allegations, or by concealment of that which should have been disclosed, which deceives and is intended to deceive another, and thereby causes injury to that person.

Home Study—A process through which prospective adoptive parents are educated about adoption and evaluated to determine their suitability to adopt.

Home Study Preparer—Any party licensed or otherwise authorized under the law of the state of the adopted child's proposed residence to conduct the research and preparation for a home study.

Identifying Information—Information on birth parents that discloses their identities.

Incapable of Providing Proper Care—Refers to a situation where the sole or surviving parent is unable to provide for the child's basic needs.

Independent Adoption—An adoption facilitated by those other than caseworkers associated with an agency including attorneys, physicians, or other intermediaries.

International Adoption—The adoption of a child who is a citizen of one country by adoptive parents who are citizens of a different country.

Interstate Compact on Adoption and Medical Assistance—An agreement between member states that governs the interstate delivery of and payment for medical services and adoption assistance subsidies for adopted children with special needs.

Interstate Compact on the Placement of Children—An agreement regulating the placement of children across state lines.

Legal Aid—A national organization established to provide legal services to those who are unable to afford private representation.

Legal Custody—The assumption of responsibility for a minor by an adult under the laws of the state and under the order or approval of a court of law or other appropriate government entity.

Legally Free—A child whose birth parents' rights have been legally terminated so that the child is "free" to be adopted by another family.

Legal Risk Placement—Placement of a child in a prospective adoptive family when a child is not yet legally free for adoption.

Matching—The process of finding prospective families specifically suited to meet the needs of a waiting child, not to be confused with "placement."

Non-Identifying Information—Facts about the birth parents or adoptive parents that would not lead to their discovery by another person.

Non-Recurring Adoption Costs—One-time adoption expenses.

Open Adoption—An adoption that involves some amount of initial and/or ongoing contact between birth and adoptive families, ranging from sending letters through the agency, to exchanging names, and/or scheduling visits.

Orphan—A minor child whose parents have died, have relinquished their parental rights, or whose parental rights have been terminated by a court of jurisdiction.

Parens Patriae—Legal term that defines the State's legal role as the guardian to protect the interests of children who cannot take care of themselves.

Paternity Testing—Genetic testing that can determine the identity of the biological father. Paternity testing can be done with or without access to the biological mother.

Placement Date—The time at which the child comes to live with the adopting parents.

Putative Father—Legal term for the alleged or supposed father of a child.

Putative Father Registries—Registry system that serves to ensure that a birth father's rights are protected.

Relinquishment—Voluntary termination of parental rights.

Reunion—A meeting between birthparent(s) and an adopted adult or between an adopted adult and other birth relatives.

Search—An attempt, usually by a birth parent, adopted person, or adoptive parent, to make a connection between the birth parent and the biological child.

Search and Consent Procedures—Procedures that authorize a public or private agency to assist a searching party to locate another party to the adoption to determine if the second party agrees to the release of identifying information or to meeting with the requesting party.

Semi-Open Adoption—An adoption in which a child's birth parents and pre-adoptive parents may exchange primarily non-identifying information.

Statute—A law.

Stepparent Adoption—The adoption of a child by the new spouse of the birth parent.

Surrender—Voluntary termination of parental rights.

Surrender Papers—Legal document attesting to the signator's voluntary relinquishment of parental rights to a child.

Surviving Parent—The child's living parent when the child's other parent is dead.

Termination of Parental Rights—The legal process which involuntarily severs a parent's rights to a child.

Traditional Adoption—Most often used to refer to a domestic infant adoption in which confidentiality is preserved.

Unconstitutional—Refers to a statute which conflicts with the United States Constitution rendering it void.

Voluntary Adoption Registry—A reunion registry system which allows adoptees, birth parents, and biological siblings to locate each other if they wish by maintaining a voluntary list of adoptees and birth relatives.

Ward—A person over whom a guardian is appointed to manage his or her affairs.

Witness—One who testifies to what he has seen, heard, or otherwise observed.

BIBLIOGRAPHY AND
ADDITIONAL READING

Adoptive Families Magazine (Date Visited: September 2007) http://www.adoptivefamiliesmagazine.com/.

American Academy of Adoption Attorneys (Date Visited: September 2007) http://www.adoptionattorneys.org/ AAAA/.

Black's Law Dictionary, Fifth Edition. St. Paul, MN: West Publishing Company, 1979.

Bureau of Citizenship and Immigration Services (BCIS) (Date Visited: September 2007) http://www.immigration.gov/.

Child Welfare Information Gateway (Date Visited: September 2007) http://www.childwelfare.gov/.

The Evan B. Donaldson Adoption Institute (Date Visited: September 2007) http://www.adoptioninstitute.org/.

Legal Information Institute, Cornell University Law School (Date Visited: September 2007) http://www.law.cornell.edu/topics/adoption.html/.

National Council For Adoption (Date Visited: September 2007) http://www.ncfa-usa.org/home.html/.

United States Department of Justice, Bureau of Citizenship and Immigration Services, Department of Homeland Security (Date Visited: September 2007)
http://ins.usdoj.gov/.

United States Department of State, Bureau of Consular Affairs (Date Visited: September 2007) http://travel.state.gov/.

United States Department of State, Office of Children's Issues (Date Visited: September 2007) http://travel.state.gov/adopt.html.